LIMERICK CITY LIBRARY

Phone: (061) 407510
Website: www.limerickcity.ie
Email: citylib@limerickcity.ie

The Granary,
Michael Street,
Limerick

This book is issued subject to the Rules of this Library.
The Book must be returned not later than the last date stamped below.

Class No. ....927-9672...... Acc. No. ....C 13400....

Date of Return	Date of Return	Date of Return	Date of Return
03. MAY 08			

Niki Lauda
The Rebel

Printing in France by Imprimerie Clerc.
Bound in France by S.I.R.C.
Photo engraving done in Switzerland by Actual Sàrl.

ISBN 2-84707-063-X

Niki Lauda
The Rebel

by

Pierre Ménard and Jacques Vassal

English version translated and edited by
David Waldron

Illustrations
Pierre Ménard

Photographs
LAT (unless otherwise stated)

Coordination
Cyril Davillerd

Dummy
Cyril Davillerd

Layout
Cyril Davillerd, Solange Amara, Anouck Monachon

Contents

Niki LAUDA

• **1**_The Austrian parliament designed by the Danish architect, Theophil von Hansen, was built in the XIXth century. It was a monument to the glorious past of an empire that was broken up after W.W.I.
(DR)

Chapter 1
1900-1970
Yesterday's world

The great Austrian writer, Stefan Zweig (who died in Brazil in 1942) described the Vienna of his childhood and youth as "Yesterday's world." It was a Vienna and an Austria very different to the ones in which Andreas Nikolaus "Niki" Lauda would grow up. This, however, was not the case for his grandparents and thousands of their contemporaries who lived in a world on which to coin a phrase 'the sun would never set:' and above all, as Zweig underlined in "Yesterday's world" without imagining that one day it would all collapse like a house of cards.

On the eve of World War I Vienna, a prosperous town of some two-and-a-half million citizens was the capital of the Austro-Hungarian Empire made up of around fifty million people. The Habsbourg family of Swiss German origins had reigned over this part of central Europe for centuries making Vienna not only its capital and place of residence but also a natural bridge between Eastern and Western Europe. The city, founded by the Celts, was then occupied by the Romans who built a military camp there and in the third century it already counted some 15,000 to 20,000 inhabitants. It was christened Venia in the Middle Ages and was a stage town for crusaders on the way to Byzantium as well as a port for the Ottoman Empire. In 1365, Rudolph IV of the Habsbourg line founded the first German language university in the city. The Gothic cathedral of Saint-Etienne built in 1433 symbolised its central importance in the Christian context. Vienna was further enriched by Renaissance style palaces but in 1683 it was partially destroyed by the Turks who had already occupied Hungary.

It was rebuilt and redeveloped in the XVIIIth century with palaces like that of the Aristocrats and churches, notably Saint-Charles-Borromée, in a baroque style, and became a cultural and musical capital that played a defining role in the lives of great composers like Mozart, Beethoven, Haydn, Bruckner, Schubert and Hugo Wolf. By the middle of the XIXth century Vienna had again become a major political centre and its religious and cultural influence was felt throughout Europe. In music the famous waltzes composed by Johan Strauss (father and son) gave the capital worldwide renown as in popular imagination they conjured up images of elegantly dressed aristocrats dancing in beautiful ballrooms in sumptuous palaces on the banks of the "blue" Danube!

In 1848, Arch Duke Francis Joseph, who had just risen to the throne, decided to replace the old ramparts by a wide circular ring road some four kilometres long along which pseudo-antique buildings were constructed that separated the heart of the historic city from the suburbs. Influenced by its musicians and the poet Rainer Maria Rilke the Vienna of yesteryear was fashioned for the next fifty years or so although the bourgeoisie thought it would go on for ever. The city became the scene of lavish receptions and servants abounded often staying with the same family for several generations. Gold coins were used to settle purchases and the 'right crowd' rubbed shoulders on church porches or in ballrooms. Soldiers back from the army married young ladies through alliances that were frequently of an economic nature having beforehand learned the tricks of the trade from prostitutes. When the males of the species were bored or had free time they sat in the famous Vienna cafes and read newspapers, then discussed current affairs such as the Austro-Hungarian Empire's annexation of Bosnia-Herzegovina in 1908. At the end of the XIXth century a modern avant-gardiste culture flourished on this very conservative soil which culminated in the brilliant Vienna school of art led by Gustav Klimt, Oskar Kokoshka and Egon Schiele aided and abetted by architects like Otto Wagner, Adolf Loos and Josef Hoffman who sculpted the face of the capital in those golden years. Around Vienna its orchestra and opera the careers of Gustav Mahler (died in 1911) then Arnold Schoenberg and Anton Webern (leader of the dodecaphonic movement) flourished. Stefan Zweig and Robert Musil were among its best-known writers in the 20s and 30s and of course, it is the city forever associated with the famous Doctor Freud whose psychoanalytical theories represent one of the major revolutions of 20th century thought. After WW II Thomas Bernhardt became the country's most important poet and playwright.

This World of Yesteryear although rich with its men of tomorrow collapsed on an historic date where Austria's history became irrevocably linked with that of the world. On 28th June 1914 the Arch Duke François-Ferdinand, heir to the throne, was assassinated in Sarajevo precipitating the empire and in its wake the rest of Europe into the most destructive war mankind had ever seen. The Habsbourgs fell in 1918 and the empire was broken up by the treaties signed in the forest of Saint-Germain-en-Laye in France in 1919, which recognised the independence of the nation states of the former double monarchy. All that remained was an area of some 83,500 kms^2 where the Austrian Republic was proudly proclaimed in 1920. It had a federal constitution and consisted of 9 provinces. Socialist and conservative parties swapped power in times of financial hardship that resulted in a civil war in 1934. The outcome of this was a brief right-wing dictatorship under Chancellor Dollfuss - assassinated on the orders of the Nazis. Then in 1938, Adolf Hitler, who never stopped reminding the world that he was Austrian, proclaimed the Anchluss or annexation of Austria by Nazi Germany with the blessing of the Catholic Church hierarchy. This led to fierce

repression of any form of opposition from trade unionists, intellectuals and progressive thinkers many of whom fled the country and of course, the Jews. Freud died in exile in London in 1939 and Wilhem Reich (who had published "The Mass Psychology of Fascism" in 1933) immigrated to the USA.

In 1945, when the Allies liberated Austria the country – like Germany – was split up into English, American, Soviet and French zones. Vienna rose slowly from its ashes: in 1951, for example it had a million inhabitants fewer than in 1914. In 1955, when Niki Lauda was a 6-year-old boy Austria was once again allowed to govern itself provided it remained neutral. Catholicism remained the majority religion (88% between the 60s and 80s) and both right and left swapped power under politicians like Bruno Kreisky and Kurt Waldheim who, before becoming Austrian chancellor, was secretary of the United Nations for a long time. These were the years when Austria developed its tourist industry, in particular in the area of winter sports and the Winter Olympics were held there twice. So the best-known sportsmen abroad were skiers beginning with Toni Seiler who, in 1956 in Cortina d'Ampezzo, won three gold medals in downhill skiing and the slalom. Then came Karl Schrantz but in the 70s he fell victim to the war on professionalism waged by the Olympics Committee. He was succeeded by Franz Klammer winner of the gold medal in Innsbruck in 1976, and more recently the incredible Hermann Maier who did the downhill sprint double in Nagano in 1998 and made a winning comeback in 2003 after a very serious motor bike accident.

And what about motor sport? In 1961 in a country that numbered only 7.5 millions inhabitants it was fairly popular thanks to a technical heritage and a top level sporting tradition, which could not have failed to fire the enthusiasm of young Niki Lauda. It is perhaps a little known fact that the young Ferdinand Porsche from Carinthia in the south of the country first showed his inventiveness when working for the Austrian company, Lohner. He built the Lohner-Porsche which had four-wheel drive as it was powered by four electric engines, one in each wheel! Then there was also the Austro-Daimler firm whose range in 1910 and the 20s included luxury and sports cars: it too employed Ferdinand Porsche. He was an independent and authoritarian man of unbending character, who changed companies on a regular basis before finding his niche. In 1924, he left Austro-Daimler and Austria for Mercedes where he developed various models including the 600 K after the merger between Mercedes and Benz in 1926. Then, after walking out on the Stuttgart firm in 1927 he set up his own design office working for different manufacturers as well as elaborating his own projects, one of which was the famous rear-engined Auto Union GP car that he designed with the help of his son Ferry II. Between 1934 and 1937 the A, B and C type Auto Unions powered by a V16 engine and then the D-Types in V12 form in 1938 and 1939 dominated grand prix racing with Mercedes-Benz. A special version enabled Hans Stuck to win – among others – the Grossglockner hill climb in the Austrian Alps near the mountain of the same name.

Another vehicle from Ferdinand Porsche's studio was a small popular car that he tried to sell in various forms to established manufacturers like Mercedes-Benz and Wanderer. Following an in-depth redesign it resurfaced as the "Kdf Wagen" which then became Volkswagen under a special agreement with Adolf Hitler and the third Reich government. Construction began in 1938 and the little Beetle served as the basis (platform, torsion bar suspension and flat 4-cylinder air-cooled engine) for the future Porsche 356. Ferdinand Porsche was imprisoned in France and liberated in 1946. His next venture was the Cisitalia project initiated by an Italian industrialist, Piero Dusio. It was a rear-engined F1 car powered by a 1500 cc supercharged engine, which never raced due to financial problems. In 1948, Ferry Porsche and a small team set up a workshop destined to assemble the first Porsche 356s in Gmünd in the Austrian Alps beside the German border. Ferdinand Porsche died in 1951 just as the eponymous make was starting to make a name for itself. Production really took off in the 50s after a move to a new site in Zuffenhausen (a Stuttgart suburb) although the German company retained close links with Austria. Numerous Austrian drivers showed their skills in Porsches and in the 60s Porsche Austria had its own endurance team, which raced 908s and 917s. Its most famous driver was Helmut Marko who won the 1971 Le Mans 24 Hours in the Martini Racing 917 purchased from Porsche Austria at the end of 1970.

Hill climbing had long been an Austrian speciality and in the 50s and 60s several rounds of the European Championship were held there in addition to Germany, Switzerland, Italy and France. Abarth, Ferrari and Porsche were the principal makes involved in the struggle for victory and among the drivers were Austrians like Johannes Ortner.

Circuitwise Formula 2 races were organised on the Vienna-Aspern track laid out on an aerodrome plus the odd non-championship F1 event and among the winners was Stirling Moss. The first Austrian Grand Prix counting for the F1 World Championship was held in 1964 on the Zeltweg military aerodrome near Graz, with victory going to Italian Lorenzo Bandini in a Ferrari. The concrete runways played havoc with suspensions and several cars were eliminated by breakages. The race also saw the grand prix debut of a young Austrian called Jochen Rindt in a Brabham-BRM. The next Austrian Grand Prix counting for the F1 Championship took place on 16th August 1970 on the magnificent Österreichring circuit laid out in a beautiful natural site near Zeltweg. Both drivers and spectators loved it.

Strangely enough it was also Jochen Rindt's last grand prix. He had become one of the greats of the era especially after Jim Clark's death in 1968 and was the first Austrian to win the F1 World Championship. His fiery temperament allied to a prize-fighter's face with its slightly battered profile enflamed the hearts of his fellow-countrymen as well as crowds abroad. He raced in sports prototypes winning the 1965 Le Mans 24 Hours with Masten Gregory in the NART entered Ferrari 250 LM and drove Brabham-Fords for Brit Roy Winklemann in F2 dominating the category. In 1965 he signed a contract with John Cooper and in 1966 and 67 he showed tremendous talent in the big, unwieldy 3-litre V12 Cooper-Maseratis before moving to Brabham in 1968 and Lotus in 1969. He did not like the 72, which he considered a dangerous car, and his fears were proved right in 1970 the year in which he won the championship. He was killed in it during practice for the Italian Grand Prix on the Monza circuit the same year making him the only man to be awarded the title posthumously. His death marked the collective Austrian memory as well as that of Niki Lauda who, nonetheless, pursued his aim to be a racing driver. He was to become the natural successor to the great Austrian who had disappeared from the grand prix scene all too prematurely. ■

Chapter 2
1949-1967
The Rebel

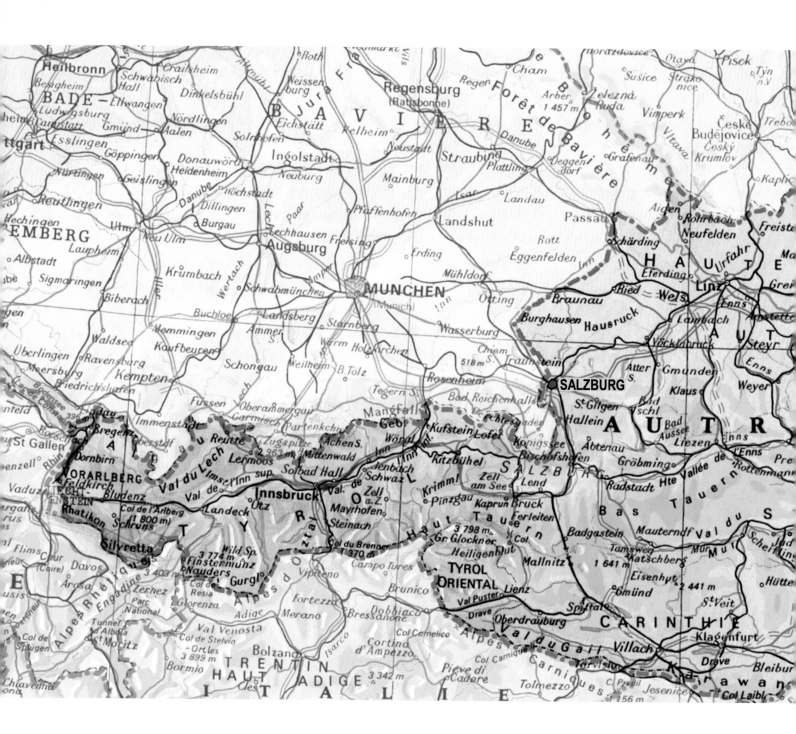

• 3_ Austria in 1984 when Niki Lauda won his third F1 Drivers' World Championship. The Aspern circuit on the aerodrome on which he made his racing debut can be seen in the Vienna suburbs. To the west near the German border is Salzburg, his adopted town, and to the south in the Styrian mountains are the small village of Zeltweg and the famous Oesterreichring.
(Reader's Digest selection)

With few exceptions most people need to belong to a group which enables them to express who and what they are. If the group in question is part of the elite the person has a much wider scope for self-expression than a member of the downtrodden masses. The approval of the group requires the acceptance of certain modes of behaviour, which enable the former to function efficiently. Refusing these rules leads to marginalisation and the more or less open hostility of the group, and also rejection of the latter's help can turn the person into a maverick! Few have the courage in such a situation to turn their back on the comfort and facilities offered to remain true to their ideas or their way of seeing life. Andreas Nicolaus Lauda is certainly one of them.

In post-war Austria whose flourishing economic growth was closely linked to that of its overbearing German neighbour, the name Lauda was already well known. It appeared in the economic rather than the sporting columns of the country's newspapers. The family was highly respected and had made its fortune in the paper industry. Convention and rigour were the leitmotifs of the Laudas who could not imagine any future for their

He was brought up with his brother Florian (born in 1950) in the comfortable and opulent surroundings befitting a well-off family but he soon rejected the advantages that his milieu offered him. He felt ill at ease and found his main pleasure in the charm of the superb properties belonging to his father and grandfather. He was a puny looking little boy who did not like sport and the one he had to do sent cold shivers down his spine. Horse riding and the grand Austrian families went hand in glove and despite his visceral aversion to anything vaguely resembling a stable, from time to time he found himself seated astride a thoroughbred trying to learn the basic technique of riding. Much later he would overcome his fear of them when he had to saddle the ones on his private property on Ibiza. This shows one of his main characteristics: he would only stick to something if it served some purpose in his life. It was the same thing at school. Straight away he was labelled a bad student who was completely bored by study and it got increasingly worse as the years wore on as he admits himself: *"I've never really understood the use of teaching, especially when I turned twelve the moment I became passionately interested in cars."* He was a bit of a dunce and only showed his capacity for learning when the need arose. For example, when the international aspect of motor racing assumed growing importance he showed himself to be a dab hand at mastering languages. So from an early age Niki Lauda rebelled against any form of indoctrination and affirmed his quirkiness plus his determination to be himself. This attitude is perfectly illustrated by the following anecdote: one day he saw his grandfather, Ernst Lauda, who was usually violently anti-socialist, being awarded a decoration by a member of the socialist government of the time. He was taken aback by this behaviour, which, to his young way for thinking, was completely illogical and sent his grandfather a letter reproaching him for not acting in accordance with his principles. This caused a major upset in the family shocked by such impudence, and he later admitted that it confirmed his feeling of not belonging to the Lauda clan. He now knew that he could only count on himself to fulfil his aims: if indeed, he ever would!

progeny other than continuing the lineage; especially not anything of a futile and frivolous nature that was not in keeping with the smooth, unruffled image that they projected in Austrian society. Andreas Nicolaus was born on 22nd February 1949 and his destiny was laid down from birth. He would be moulded in such a way as to make of him a worthy representative of the dynasty, namely, a young well-mannered, elegant Viennese as much at home on the dance floor as on horseback whose success as a student would enable him to become a diligent member of the family industrial tribe. To the dismay of his parents, Ernst-Peter and Elisabeth, Niki soon showed that he was a square peg in a round hole.

(*) "300 km/h" See bibliography at the end of the book.

Despite his steely determination to shake off the family mantle, the "family fridge" as he called it, his future looked bleak. He was placed in a strict school that was supposed to provide him with his leaving certificate but felt no attraction for what the industrial life had to offer, and especially not this stupid exam, which appeared to have absolutely no bearing on his ambitions. The only thing that attracted him was the automobile.

Early on Niki was fascinated by the beautiful cars of the guests who came to his grandfather's estate (the latter owned a Jaguar). He appointed himself as a parking attendant and people who were only too happy to let him park their cars so he was able to manoeuvre them to his heart's content for a whole evening. When he was obliged to hand back the keys after the party was over he felt a bit like Cinderella on the stroke of midnight and decided to get his own car at the age of fifteen! He saved up 1500 schillings (around 60 euros at the time) and bought himself a Volkswagen coupe, which was the same age as him but in a rather more dilapidated condition. At the wheel of his beetle he raced up and down the alleys of his father's property, and then when he was fed up with its confines had the car transported to his grandfather's demesne on whose private roads he could drive like a madman. He was very interested in the mechanical aspects and took the car apart to see how it worked. Maybe that was why one day his parents exasperated by his dreadful school results and his love of grease, got him an apprenticeship as a mechanic in a garage. And so at seventeen the young heir to the famous Lauda dynasty found himself on the tram on his way to work early in the morning like any Austrian labourer. His initial happiness at his newfound freedom soon gave way to fresh misgivings.

His dreams of nuts and bolts soon came up against the harsh reality of daily work in a garage. He did not really feel very concerned by the maintenance of the cars entrusted to him and mistakes piled up. In fact, he was demoted to the rank of coffee and sausage boy! After a year of this treatment Niki realised that he had taken the wrong path and began evening courses to pass his leaving certificate, which, it seemed, was the first step on the road to happiness and prosperity. Another blunder! He discovered that he could not go against his own desires and all these ups and downs were beginning to get under his skin. He made up his mind to become a racing driver and decided to get the wherewithal to do it. He was motivated by his parents' promise of a cash reward if he passed his exam and tricked them into believing he had done so by forging his name on a girlfriend's certificate. Thus, he was given enough money to enable him to buy a Volkswagen that was a tiny bit quicker than his first one.

All he knew about racing was what he had seen and read. Like any enthusiast he devoured specialised magazines and went to circuits like Vienna-Aspern and the Nürburgring in Germany where he was enthralled by the sight of cars going flat out side-by-side from corner to corner. He loved speed but did not identify with any of the modern day heroes who haunted the dreams of their fans. Like many great sportsmen his only idol was himself. He was not insensitive to the growing charisma of Jochen Rindt as the latter was starting to fan the flames of his fellow-countrymen's enthusiasm but never did he pin his posters on his bedroom wall. He did not dream of becoming one of the greats as his only aim was to race and prove that he was the best in an area he had deliberately chosen. Of course, this crazy idea was not mentioned in the family, which was under the impression that now that he had passed his exam he would at last put his nose to the grindstone. One winter's night in 1968 fate was to take a hand in his destiny giving him a foretaste of what was to come until he joined Ferrari in 1973.

He was driving flat out on the Vienna boulevards in a Mini-Cooper S borrowed from a friend's father and learned the hard way the effect of ice on a car travelling at full speed. The result was sudden contact with a bridge parapet and one very modified Mini. The car was up for sale and Niki had no other choice than to buy it before its owner saw the state of the apple of his eye, and took the necessary legal steps to punish the person responsible for the car's involuntary redesign! He got the money thanks to the indulgence of his paternal grandmother

who lent him the amount asked by the seller. Thus, his "stable" now included a badly damaged Mini Cooper and a clapped out Volkswagen plus a debt of 38 000 schillings. The only way to reimburse his debt was to race in the hope of winning the prize money on offer for good results. Lauda chose a Mini-Cooper in racing trim sold by the king of the speciality, Fritz Baumgartner. He sold his Volkswagen to pay for repairs to the crashed Mini, which was traded off against the racing version and took on additional debts to complete the transaction. Baumgartner impressed by his determination and also by the financial resources of his family, offered to look after him. ■

• 4_In this photo taken in his parents' garden in 1970 a 'butter wouldn't melt in my mouth' Lauda looks like an obedient son, a role he soon rejected. He made a name for himself thanks to his stubbornness that sometimes bordered on rashness.
(Alois Rottensteiner)

Chapter 3
1968–1970
Survival
of the fittest

Lauda's racing debut on 15th April 1968 at
the wheel of his 1300 cc Mini-Cooper in
the Bad Mühllacken hill climb came in a
special atmosphere. Obviously, he was very
excited about something that would have a
decisive effect on his future but overshadowing
it all was Jim Clark's fatal accident in an F2 race
on the Hockenheim circuit the week before. In
that era motor racing was a lot more dangerous
than it is today and death was not selective in
its choice of victims. On this occasion the grim
reaper had taken the most gifted and the most
charismatic drivers of his generation whom
everybody thought invincible so great was his
mastery of his art. Lauda was not demoralized
by the news but felt somehow that this
exceptional individual had paid the highest
price possible in a sport, which he was about
to tackle for the first time. Once he was behind
the wheel he channelled all his thoughts into
doing his best in the test that awaited him.
Already he was reacting in the cold-blooded
way of a true racer by eliminating from his
mind anything that might interfere with his
concentration. Niki ended up third quickest
after nursing his engine. Fritz Buamgartner

told him that he could up the revs and in the
second climb he was fastest which gave him
second place overall. However, his homecoming
was not exactly greeted with thunderous
applause. Baumgartner had spilled the beans to
Ernst-Peter Lauda who told Niki in no uncertain
terms to abandon his dream of carving out a
career for himself at the wheel of a racing car.
This was just the goad that his stubborn
offspring needed to break off relations with
his family. Ten days later he entered for the
Dobratsch hill climb and won. He followed this
up with another couple of victories in the Alpl
and Engelhartszel events, which gave him
a budding reputation and a little cash that
would help to fund future projects.

As he had now been thrown out by his
family (he would not resume normal relations
with his parents until after his accident at
the 'Ring in 1976) he set up home in Salzburg
with his girlfriend of the moment, Mariela
Reininghaus, and swapped his Mini for a
Porsche 911 taking on more debt. He had
chosen his life style with his eyes wide open,
which was just the opposite of the way he
had behaved up to then. He lived in a little

apartment and the whole of his modest income was invested in racing. He continued in hill climbs and also did a few circuit events in his Porsche 911 which was immaculately prepared in the workshop of hill climb specialist Gerhard Mitter, European Champion in 1966, 67 and 68. Out of nine events (hill climbs and circuits) Niki won five (including one on the Zeltweg aerodrome scene of the first Austrian F1 GP in 1964) finished third and then eighth and retired twice. The pundits of the day said that young Lauda was not a particularly gifted driver but his determination and racing science were impressive. In addition, he was obsessed with perfection especially in the top class preparation of his car, something that cost money but which was worth it from his point of view even if it plunged him deeper in debt. As his results had

• **7**_For young drivers Formula V was an excellent launching pad to more prestigious formulas. Thanks to his 2 victories in 1969 Lauda hoped that new horizons would open up for him.
(Josef Mayrhofer)

• **8**_Niki was eager to try his hand at any form of racing especially when it brought him good starting and prize money, which he used to finance his career. In 1969, he drove the agile Porsche 910 powered by a 2-litre flat-6 engine and he finished 21st on the new Osterreichring with fellow-countryman Stuppacher.
(Josef Mayrhofer)

• **9**_In 1970, he launched himself on the F3 scene with his compatriot Gerold Plankl with whom he had battled in Formula V the previous year. (Alois Rottensteiner)

earned him substantial prize money and a growing notoriety he decided to take up single-seater racing.

He caught the eye of Kurt Bergmann who managed a team in the Formula V Championship. At the end of 1968 Lauda tested one of his Kaimanns and signed with him for 1969. He finished eighth in his first single-seater race in October 1968 on the Vienna-Aspern track where he also came third in his Porsche 911 the same day. Formula V – a purely German category – offered a debutant the immediate opportunity to race in international events whose technical, sporting and financial level was below that of Formula 3. The cars were simple, small and light and not very powerful and no-holds barred scraps between the drivers were commonplace. In April 1969 he finished in an encouraging fourth place in his first race at

Hockenheim but in the next race on the Vienna-Aspern track he had a big accident. His no.7 Kaimann flew into the air and fortunately for him landed upside down on the grass verge bordering the track. He was knocked out but far from demoralised. *"I was completely crazy, hungry for victory and without a moment's thought I tried to overtake where it just wasn't on."* Despite this he began to notch up promising results, second in Belgrade, fourth in Budapest and then back to Hockenheim where he came second. He could have scored his first win after a bitter duel with his fellow-countryman, Erich Breinsberg, as he was leading on the last lap but the latter took him by surprise in the Stadium corner and snatched victory. Two races later he saw the chequered flag for the first time in Sopron, a Hungarian town not far from the Austrian border.

(*) "300 km/h" See bibliography at the end of the book.

He had to wait until the last race on the Munich-Neubiberg aerodrome to score his second victory. In the meantime he underlined his reputation as a steady driver with a couple of second places on the Nürburgring and at Innsbruck and two thirds at Tulin-Langeulebarn and on the Salzburgring. He retired only once due to mechanical problems. Helmut Marko, 0a fellow Austrian who was older and more experienced than Lauda, raced against him in a McNamara (he later drove for BRM in Formula 1 in 1971 and 72) and noticed that Niki used his intelligence much more than the bunch of mad dogs that made up most of the field. He reconnoitred the track beforehand and analysed all its ups and downs, a singular attitude in a milieu not noted for its powers of reflection. Already he was extremely organised and methodical, two qualities that were the keys to his rigorous way of doing things which would lay the foundations of his future world championship successes. In 1970, his intelligence and analytical sense were to be sorely tested.

At the end of his second season which was pretty good overall without being exceptional he continued learning his trade in single-seaters, the pinnacle of the sport and the path to further glory, especially for a young Austrian. At the end of 1969 Jochen Rindt had proved just how good he was by winning the USA Grand Prix in his Gold Leaf Lotus 49 and became a hero for a whole nation. When he was doing a presentation in Vienna-Aspern he shook the numerous hands that reached out to him from the crowd including Niki Lauda's. It was the only contact between two men from different generations, separated by their age and above all by Rindt's death at Monza in 1970.

Morally speaking Lauda was in fine fettle (the same could not be said for his finances) as he set about organising his 1970 season, this time in Formula 3. He was still alone and received little help so he had to borrow more money to buy the McNamara to take on the best young drivers on the international scene. He had to do everything himself like towing his car, a large borrowed BMW, to the circuits

• **10**_Before the start of the Brands Hatch race in July 1970 Lauda told photographer, Alois Rottensteiner, that Clearways was the ideal spot to take a good photo of a driver who had gone off. Little did he know that the person in question would be himself!
(Alois Rottensteiner)

• **11**_He was fed up with the crazy world of F3 and decided to finish his 1970 season driving the sports prototype Porsche 908. On the Österreichring in October he finished 6ᵗʰ.

resulting in long and difficult journeys, sleep and eat where and when he could while keeping all his energy intact for the race.

Alas, his F3 season turned into a nightmare. This could be attributed to the accumulation of pressure and stress allied to his barely controlled youthful hotheadedness, as he seemed ready to do battle with all comers whatever the cost. His first race was on the Nogaro circuit at the end of March 1970 and with barely five minutes gone he took off over the back of his fellow countryman, Gerold Pankl's car, and ended up in the greenery. Thirty-six hours on the road for nothing. In May he finished fifth at Magny-Cours but then crashed again a week later at Hockenheim. He came sixth on the new Österreichring

inaugurated the previous year followed by a second place in Brun in Czechoslovakia and it looked like he had learned his lesson. No way as he went off all by himself in the first corner on the Brands Hatch circuit in July. Worse was to come at the beginning of September at Zolder where he found himself in the middle of the field and was involved in a 200 km/h pile-up at the start of the race. He was stuck in his badly damaged McNamara as cars flew by on either side their drivers paying no heed to the yellow flags. Although scared stiff he managed to clamber out of the wreck and run away.

In 1966, Jackie Stewart had endured deep psychological torture in the remains of his overturned BRM on the Spa circuit as petrol seeped into the cockpit and he was terrified that

practice for the Italian Grand Prix the day before the F3 race at Zolder certainly weighed heavily, psychologically speaking, in his decision. He immediately stopped racing in F3 and gave himself the time to think calmly about how to find the means to continue in single-seaters the following year against more mature drivers. However, among the wild men in F3 he had made friends with an Englishman who was two years older than him, already had a reputation as a bit of a lad and drove like a maniac sometimes with his eyes closed. The guy in question was James Hunt and in fact he won the race on the Zolder circuit. He was drawn to the young Austrian's forceful character. The two men got to know each other well and they lived together in London during the lean years. Much later on they fought a memorable duel that made headlines all over the world and they always held each other in the greatest respect.

While Niki Lauda did not know what 1971 held he still had some sports car racing to do. The year before he had driven an Opel 1900 on two occasions (two retirements) and this year he found himself behind the wheel of a Porsche 908, a very different animal. In it he learned how to master power as its flat 6 engine put out around 350 bhp giving himself good experience. The races also enabled him to win considerable prize money, which came in handy for paying a part of his future single-seater projects. Out of eight races he won two non-championship events in sports prototypes in the Bosch Team's 908 at Diepholz in July and on the Österreichring in late October when he also raced in a round of the Sports Car World Championship on the same circuit partnered by fellow-countryman Peter. They finished sixth. His ambitions, though, still revolved around single-seaters and for 1971 he began to think about taking a big step up to F2. Its main advantage was that it was a doorway to F1 and provided the opportunity to race against some of the best F1 drivers who competed in F2 as well as their world championship programme. The major drawback was its cost especially for someone like Lauda who had not exactly set the world on fire in the lower formulas. Small loans from well-intentioned benefactors were no longer any use as the price of a season was way beyond the means of a young, penniless driver without headline grabbing results. He was to change status from that of an amateur to being a fully-fledged professional in every sense of the term. ■

a fire would start. The lesson that the Scot drew from that accident was that himself and his fellow-drivers were not paid to kill themselves but to compete in maximum safety. He changed his vision of racing trying to reduce the dangerous aspect of his profession to the minimum possible by using his brain rather than his balls! This change of attitude did not prevent him from driving some exceptional races. Lauda too thought about what he had been through. "This was when I began to call on some of my talents that had been neglected or ignored up till then such as thinking or setting myself an aim. The result was as follows: yes I wanted to race, that was undeniable but I didn't want to be a wild man among other wild men."* Even though Lauda denies it Jochen Rindt's death in

(*) "300 km/h" See bibliography at the end of the book.

Chapter 4
*1971–1972
What's he
doing in
Formula 1?*

• **13**_This photo symbolises the bad luck that pursued him in Formula 2 in 1971. He either finished at the back of the field or fell foul of mechanical problems as illustrated by this broken right-hand front wishbone on his March 712.
(DPPI)

At the start of 1971 Niki Lauda decided to contact the fledgling March outfit after assessing his options for the year in question. It had been founded in March 1969 by Alan Rees, Graham Coaker, Robin Herd and Max Mosley who looked after its management thanks to his training as a lawyer. He was a dab hand at selling his future clients the idea of a team that was capable of providing competitive cars whether in F1, F2 or F3. At the end of the 1970 season the results were not quite as good as expected but nonetheless boded well for the future. In F1 Jackie Stewart gave the team its first grand prix victory in Spain in a Tyrrell-entered 701 and in the European F2 Championship (won by Regazzoni's Tecno) Swedish hope Ronnie

Peterson finished a promising fourth overall. Lauda thought that joining a team involved in both F1 and F2 would enable him to show his talent and fulfil his ambitions so he met Mosley at the end of 1970.

On this occasion Niki used his Viennese family connections as Mosley too came from a privileged background and was thus sensitive to the conventions of upper-class social intercourse. They took to each other immediately but getting round the harsh reality of money was another story, and the upshot of it all was that if Niki wanted to have the no.2 seat behind Ronnie Peterson he had to pay as Max Mosley recalls: *"It was clear that he had to be a pay driver as he had no results to speak of. He had done almost*

no Formula 3 and gave no real indication that he was a champion in the making." An F2 seat cost around £10,000 (500,000 schillings). Niki did not hesitate for a second as he was afraid of losing his only chance to make his name and signed the contract linking him to March. Only when he had left Mosley did he start thinking think about how he would lay his hands on the 500,000 schillings that he had to pay in the next few days. His sponsor was no longer enough as Bosch was ready to pay only one-tenth of the amount. He had to find a backer with deeper pockets. Luckily the Bosch competitions manager put him in touch with a friend who was the manager of the "Erste Österreichische Sparkasse" the Austrian Savings bank which lent him the rest of the

money. Concerning all his loans it is worth remembering that the name Lauda was an excellent reference in Austria and the budding driver took advantage of his background - for once! So he was able to come up with the cash.

Niki took the opposite route to the majority of the top drivers who were recruited according to their results as he paid a lot of money in the hope of making an impression on the people who mattered. It was a high-risk strategy with failure rather than success as the most likely outcome. And it turned out to be another disastrous year for the young Austrian as out of fourteen races his best results were two sixth and one fourth place. He finished outside the points on five occasions, failed to qualify once and retired five

• **14**_His best race in 1971 came on the Rouen circuit. F2 at that time was an excellent way of matching one's skills against F1 stars. Here he is seen in the "Nouveau Monde" hairpin with Henri Pescarolo no.18, Mike Beuttler no.45 and team-mate Ronnie Peterson no.4 who won the event. *(Roland Kerdilès)*

P. MÉNARD

Designer: Robin Herd

Engine

Make/type: Ford Cosworth DHV
Number of cylinders, position: V8 (rear)
Cubic capacity: 2993 ccs
Bore/stroke: 85.6 x 64.8 mm
Compression ratio: 12;1
Max. Power: 455 bhp
Max. Revs: 10,500 rpm
Block: aluminium
Fuel/oil: STP
Plugs: Champion
Injection: Lucas
Distribution: 4 O.H.Cs
Number of valves per cylinder: 4
Ignition: Lucas
Weight: 163 kgs

Transmission

Gearbox/ no.of ratios: Hewland FG 400 (5)
Clutch: Borg & Beck

Chassis

Type: Aluminium monocoque
Suspension: Double wishbone, inboard coil springs dampers front/
lower wishbones, single top link with twin raduis arms each side
plus outboard coil spring damper units, rear
Dampers: Koni
Wheel diameters: 13" front & rear
Rims: 11" (Front) /16" (Rear)
Tyres: Goodyear
Brakes: Girling

Dimensions

Wheelbase: 2540 mm
Tracks: 1520 mm front and rear
Dry weight: 550 kgs
Fuel tank capacity: 180 litres

Used in Austria in 1971 and in Argentina and South Africa in 1972
designated 721.

times. Perhaps his sole consolation was that he was able to see how his team-mate Ronnie Peterson managed to get so much speed out of the March 712M in which he won the European F2 title that year. The only time he overtook Peterson was in the Rouen-Les-Essarts round where he scored his fourth place but he was immediately told in no uncertain terms by his pit to lift off and let the Swede back in front. Niki, however, was the first to admit that the blond Scandinavian had a real gift for driving over the limits of his car, and this pushed him to take more risks to increase his speed. The more attentive observers noticed that the Austrian had made some real progress that year but then so had several others. His wish to make a name for

himself had got off to a bad start and his performance in the F1 Grand Prix on the Osterreichring did nothing to enhance his reputation.

On the awesome Zeltweg circuit he was able to see how far he had come in three years. The rebel who had dropped everything and broken his family links was about to race with the top drivers in the world in front of his home public. But who really knew him? Wasn't he just another local hope like Helmut Marko also making his grand prix debut in a BRM? This situation was not helped by the fact that he started from twenty-first and second-last position on the grid. He was in a March 711 (paid for of course) the Alfa Romeo-engined version

with a difficult gearbox usually driven by Nanni Galli. For Lauda's debut a more flexible V8 Cosworth was installed but it was not enough to boost the young driver's confidence. The race confirmed what he had discovered in practice. He came into the pits after twenty laps struggling to keep the March on the track and declared that it was undriveable. It was an enormous disappointment for him to end his first F1 race like this. As the season wound down he realised that his whole year had been the opposite of what he had expected epitomised by his performance in his home grand prix. The responsibility was his alone as the team's star, Ronnie Peterson, who drove exactly the same car, finished second in the F1 Drivers' World

Championship albeit a long way behind Jackie Stewart. Niki's only win that year was in a Chevron-Ford in a race for 2-litre sports cars. It was not exactly the best bait to attract the major F1 team managers. Lauda coldly analysed his situation and saw there was only one solution: go for it without looking back! And against all expectations Max Mosley recontacted him. The March boss offered him an F1 programme for 1972 alongside Peterson as well as F2 but pointing out that he was not the only candidate for the seat. In fact, Mosley was being slightly economical with the truth as people were not exactly beating a path to his door so he really had little choice but to take on the Austrian as no.2 driver provided he coughed up the cash. The

• **15**_15ᵗʰ August 1971 should have been a red-letter day for Lauda as it was his first F1 grand prix and in addition in front of his home crowd on the Österreichring. His dream quickly turned to a nightmare due to his abysmal performance.

• **16**_The 1972 F2 season
got off to a good start for him.
After a 2nd place at Mallory
Park and a win at Oulton Park
he led the championship. Then
it all went wrong and he was
dogged by bad luck like here
in Pau in May where he
retired.
(DPPI)

P.MÉNARD

Designer: Robin Herd

Engine

Make/type: Ford Cosworth DFV
No. of cylinders. Position: V8 rear
Cubic capacity: 2993 ccs
Bore/stroke: 85.6 x 64.8 mm
Compression ratio: 12:1
Max/power 455 bhp
Max. revs: 10,800 rpm
Block: aluminium
Fuel/oil: STP
Plugs: Champion
Injection: Lucas
Distribution: 4 O.H.Cs
No. of valves per cylinder: 4
Ignition: Lucas
Weight: 163 kgs

Transmission

Gearbox/no. of ratios: Hewland/Alfa Romeo (5)
Clutch: Borg & Beck

Chassis

Type: Aluminium monocoque
Suspension: inboard springs front and rear
Dampers: Koni
Wheel diameter: 13" front and rear
Rim widths: 11" (Front) / 16" (Rear)
Tyres: Goodyear
Brakes: Lockheed

Dimensions

Wheelbase: 2540 mm
Tracks: 1520 mm front and rear
Dry weight: 550 kgs
Fuel tank capacity: 180 litres

Raced in France and the USA.

1971 March balance sheet showed a £70,000 deficit and the £40,000 which he asked Lauda for would make it look a whole lot healthier. Mosley confirmed to us just how critical the situation was: *"Without Lauda and the fact that his money arrived in the autumn March would've shut down. Without his dosh we wouldn't have lasted the 1971-72 winter. So you could say that Niki Lauda saved March!"* The Austrian really did not have much choice either. His enthusiasm was fired when Robin Herd told him about his new design the 721X, which was going to put the team on the front of the grid in F1. The young Austrian's main problem as always was finding the money for the coming season as well as reimbursing two-thirds of the previous loan,

around 350,000 schillings. The "Erste Österreichische" gave a favourable reply to the new plan put forward by Lauda, who was now a past master in the art of juggling with increasingly heavy debts, and agreed to let him have 2.5 million schillings. *"It was an enormous amount for the time,"* recalls Max Mosley *"and represented between 30 and 40% of an F1 team's budget."* Thanks to this backing Niki signed his contract with March for 1972 and then suddenly received the bad news that the bank's Board of Directors refused to authorise the loan.

Once he had overcome his initial shock he tried to find out who was behind the decision and quickly discovered that his grandfather, Ernst Lauda, had put pressure on the bank to cancel its

agreement in the misguided hope that it would put his grandson back on the straight and narrow. Any chance of him mending the break with his family was immediately scuppered. He reacted at once and soon found an understanding partner in the Raiffeisenkasse, which accepted to finance the sum, in question. Their relationship, which was beneficial for both parties, lasted until 1978.

Obviously, Niki was impatient to test his new weapon, the 721X, which had an Alfa Romeo gearbox fitted the 'wrong way' round between the engine and the differential in order to create a low polar moment and also a damper system that was supposed to make the Goodyear tyres (replacing the previous year's Firestones) work

better. He had a couple of mediocre drives in an interim 721 in the Argentinean and South African Grands Prix, and the eagerly awaited newcomer made its debut in the Spanish round on the Jarama circuit where in preliminary testing Ronnie equalled Jackie Stewart's reference time. The March team was over the moon but in official practice the early euphoria quickly evaporated. Peterson could only manage ninth fastest due to severe handling problems and he retired in the race. The mind-boggling times set in free practice were but an illusion. Stewart had had great difficulty in setting up his Tyrrell and was taking it easy, something which the March team somehow managed to overlook! That was what Lauda said on the evening of the race in

• 17_His 1972 F1 season with March was poisoned by the infamous 721X whose inverted rear springs can be clearly seen in this photo taken at the Spanish Grand Prix. This setback forced designer Robin Herd to pull out all the stops and come up with a new car, the 721G, which replaced the 721X after only 3 races. Niki Lauda was the only one who realised that the latter was a disaster but no one listened to him.

• **18**_The 721G was a direct derivate of the F2 722 which it resembled to a tee. On Lauda's right is Robin Herd.

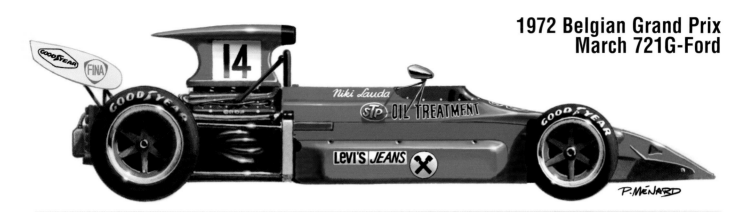

Designer: Robin Herd

Engine
Make/type: Ford Cosworth DVD
No. of cylinders/position: V8/rear
Cubic capacity: 2993 ccs
Bore/stroke: 85.6 x 64.8 mm
Compression ratio: 12:1
Max. Power: 455 bhp
Max.revs: 10,800 rpm
Block: Aluminium
Fuel/oil: STP
Plugs: Champion
Injection: Lucas
Distribution: 4 O.H.Cs
No. of valves per cylinder: 4
Ignition: Lucas
Weight: 163 kgs

Transmission
Gearbox/ no. of ratios: McLaren Hewland (5)
Clutch: Borg & Beck

Chassis
Type: Aluminium monocoque
Suspension: Inboard springs front and rear
Wheel diameters: 13 inches front and rear
Rim widths: 11 inches front, 16/17 inches rear
Tyres: Goodyear
Brakes: Girling

Dimensions
Wheelbase: 2540 mm
Tracks: 1520 mm front and rear
Dry weight: 550 kgs
Fuel tank capacity: 180 litres

Raced in Spain and Belgium.

which he was an early retirement due to a jammed accelerator pedal. He was completely discomfited. How could his team have screwed things up so badly? He could not believe how Peterson had managed to entertain the illusion for so long during practice that the 721X was a good car despite spins and off-course excursions. Who was right? He was told that he lacked experience, which he was inclined to believe, but in his heart he knew that the March was a monumental blunder designwise (see Max Mosley's sidebar). Two events later it was shelved for good and Herd got down to sketching a new F1 in record time, the 721G, which was an extrapolation of the F2 721. It was ready in nine days! It was a psychological victory for Lauda as

it confirmed his ability to analyse a car and judge each one on its merits. Even so this personal satisfaction could not mask the extremely unfavourable climate in which he was trying to shine. His F1 season with March turned out to be another disaster. The March 721G's design was a bodge job due to lack of time and when he did not retire Lauda finished way down the field. The team was having increasing problems balancing its budget and components were in short supply. In his second home grand prix he had two used tyres fitted at the front which caused the car to understeer viciously putting him on the back of the grid. The only consolation was that he finished, albeit in a lowly tenth place. By now a number of pundits were beginning to ask

• **19**_A glum Lauda reads a
magazine. The end of the 1972
season was the most critical
moment in his career. He was
up to his eyeballs in debt, had
no drive and the future looked
bleak.
(Alois Rottensteiner)

themselves what was this funny guy, who walked
like a duck and had rabbity teeth (he was later
given the nickname 'The Rat'), doing in
Formula 1.

The young Austrian had hoped to make up
for the F1 debacle by winning in F2 (in which he
was the team leader) and after the first two
events he led the European Championship
following a second at Mallory Park and a victory
at Oulton Park. Here too his hopes were dashed
as he suffered an uninterrupted series of

mechanical failures that did not end until July
when he came second in the Imola round. By
then it was too late and Mike Hailwood went on
to win the title in his Surtees-Ford. He also drove
a BMW Alpina coupe in Touring Car races
finishing third at Zandvoort and retiring at
Brünn. His season ended with the Kyalami 9-
Hour race in which he shared a March-BMW
with South African coming man Jody Scheckter:
they finished fourth. By the end of 1972 he
realised that he was far from achieving his aims

Max Mosley: "The inexperienced driver was right..."

The current president of the FIA and ex-boss of the March outfit remembers the setback of the 721X in 1972 which brought out certain qualities in Niki Lauda.
"Because he had problems with the 721X or any other car one could not say that Lauda was a bad driver. There was always a difference between Peterson and him. This was our yardstick at March. We firmly beloved that Ronnie was one of the greats of the era, and in terms of pure speed Lauda wasn't in the same ballpark. When the 721X appeared Peterson got the best out of it and didn't say much against it. Lauda stated that it was impossible to drive but we were not ready to listen to him. Then Ronnie's grid positions soon showed that the car didn't work, and we had to face the truth: it was virtually

undriveable. And Niki was the one who, right from the start, had said this. It was difficult for us, though, as on the one hand you had a driver who had little experience and had never really done any F1 claiming that the car was a dog. In addition he was a pay driver. On the other, you had someone recognised as being one of the quickest that everyone wanted and he said that we'd manage to get it working!
Niki was very determined, very intelligent and it became increasingly obvious that he had what it took to set up a car. In any case he managed to describe the car's drawbacks. Ronnie took the car as it was and thanks to his talent drove over the problems. Robin Herd really wanted to keep Lauda for 1973 as he was a great help to the engineers and not that slow either. In F2 we saw that with a good car he did the job and set more or less the same lap times as Peterson. You could have guessed from that that he would eventually get it together in Formula 1. Robin, who's a great optimist, told him that they'd do something together. He always thought that it would come right eventually and my job was to explain this to Lauda. But without money he just couldn't stay."

as Max Mosley pointed out when Lauda asked him what the future held. The figures spoke for themselves: non-classified in the F1 World Championship, fifth in F2 with one victory. His future with March might be in an F2 car but F1 was out of the question. The message was clear: Niki had missed the boat. His future looked bleak as nobody wanted to back him at this stage of his career. He had no money, was up to his eyes in debt, had no job except driving race cars which others seemed able to do much better

than him. *"Leaving Bicester where I'd had a final discussion with March, I had suicidal thoughts for the first and last time in my life,"* Lauda admitted in his memoirs. *"I had just enough time to come to my senses. A job in Civvy Street was out of the question without studies and training. Reimbursing my debts would take a lifetime. So I had no choice. I had to continue racing like before."* * This then was the somewhat topsy-turvy psychological state in which Lauda received an offer from Louis Stanley. ■

(*) "300 km/h" See bibliography at the end of the book.

Chapter 5
1973
The Wheeler
Dealer

BRM (British Racing Motors) was founded
just after WWII by Raymond Mays and
Peter Berthon. It was taken over by Sir
Alfred Owen in 1952 and had its moment of
glory in 1962 when Graham Hill won the F1
World Championship in the V8 Type 56. In 1963,
Lotus and Jim Clark began their domination but
BRM was still a force to be reckoned with.
As the years passed the team's fortunes declined
and Sir Alfred progressively handed over the
reins to his daughter Jean's husband, Louis
Stanley, and then retired. The latter was a
perfect example of an English eccentric who
took full advantage of his position and its
privileges, giving his largesse to those whom he

liked and his caustic humour to those who got
on his nerves. Alas for BRM a big question mark
hung over his competence as a manager and
the once-glorious team was slowly but surely
going down the tubes in the early 70s despite a
brief revival in 1971. It scored its last victory in
1972 when Jean-Pierre Beltoise came home first
in Monaco, a success that was down to the
qualities of the driver rather than the car's
performance. At the end of 1972 Louis Stanley,
whose main contribution to F1 was to set up
the basis of a medical service on the circuits,
found himself short of drivers and even more
importantly money as the tobacco giant,
Marlboro, was rethinking its options. Word had

Designer: Mike Pilbeam

Engine
Make/type: BRM
No. of cylinders/position: 60° V12 (rear)
Cubic capacity: 2998 ccs
Bore/stroke: 74.9 x 57.18 mm
Compression ratio: 11.5:1
Max. power: 460 bhp
Max.revs: 11,500 rpm
Block: Aluminium
Fuel/oil: Fina
Plugs: Champion
Injection: Lucas
Distribution: 4 O.H.Cs
No. of valves per cylinder: 4
Ignition: Dinoplex
Weight: -

Transmission
Gearbox/no. of ratios: BRM (5)
Clutch: -

Chassis
Type: Aluminium monocoque
Suspension: Double wishbones
Dampers: Koni
Wheel diameter: -
Rim widths: -
Tyres: Firestone
Brakes: Lockheed

Dimensions
Wheelbase: 2490 mm
Tracks: 1500 mm (Front) / 1520 mm (Rear)
Dry weight: 577 kgs
Fuel tank capacity: 204 litres

Used from Spain to the USA.

reached him that Lauda was an excellent piggy bank so he offered him an F1 seat for 1973 alongside Beltoise and Regazzoni. The latter was more than sceptical when he heard about the hiring of the young Austrian: *"Marlboro had asked me to join BRM when the team had five cars! 'It's crazy,' I said. 'I'll come and sign but no more than two cars.' And the agreement I signed with Louis Stanley stated only two cars for Beltoise and me. In December 1972, Louis Stanley ordered me to come to his suite in the Dorchester in London. He made a fine speech telling me that a young driver wanted to join us, that he had made a good proposal and so on. I answered. 'Mr Stanley, our agreement is perfectly clear. The*

contract states that there will be a maximum of two cars. You know very well that you haven't got the means to look after three.' He rambled on saying that BRM had good sponsors, and as has often happened, I allowed myself to be talked round. At Kyalami I discovered that there were five engines for three cars! For two it was OK but not for three. Niki was one too many. He can thank me because if I'd said no that day to Mr Stanley he would never have been included in the team. And his career would've been completely different."

Niki Lauda did not hesitate for a second even if BRM's reputation was more than slightly tarnished. It was his only chance of remaining in

● **23**_ Lauda really showed his talent in the streets of Monaco in 1973. He held onto 3rd place keeping Jackie Ickx's Ferrari at bay for over 20 laps. Across the Alps the old fox watched with interest.

the elite and in addition his team-mates were both experienced drivers who could teach him more about the tricks of the trade. As usual his main worry was cash, as he needed another two million schillings! This time the outlook was worse than ever as he knew that there was no way the Raiffeisenkasse would give him the money: nor any other institution for that matter. Faced with financial suffocation he suddenly had a crazy and completely irrational idea. He would lead Louis Stanley to believe that he had a sponsor ready to pay.

His plan consisted of persuading Stanley that the Reiffeisenkasse would come up with the first third of the amount just when he paid Lauda his first starting money. This moment coincided with his rewards from touring car racing. All the cunning Austrian had to do was send his prize money (banked) with the Raiffiesenkasse logo to BRM by letter and Bob's your uncle! For the rest he knew that he had to pull off something spectacular which would change his status once and for all. As one can see a lot of question marks hung over this plan which was as daring as it was mind-boggling! Then again aren't the craziest projects often the ones that have the greatest chance of success? It was under these circumstances way beyond the comprehension of ordinary mortals that Niki Lauda attacked his second full season in F1.

As soon as testing began Lauda discovered his new environment. The engineers Mike Pilbeam and Peter Windsor-Smith looked after the BRM P160's chassis and engine respectively. He particularly appreciated the driveability and sound of its V12, which was completely new to him. He quickly gained the respect of the team for his hard work and his speed. This was purely relative and the early races brought him back down to earth with a bump. The BRMs were much slower than their rivals despite Clay Regazzoni's surprise pole in the opening round of the 1973 world championship in Buenos Aires. Niki's first three races in Argentina, Brazil and South Africa yielded no points but at least he had the consolation of knowing that he was getting quicker and quicker as witnessed by his practice times. After the overseas events the circus returned to Europe for the Spanish Grand Prix (another retirement) followed by the Belgian event. It brought back bad memories for

Lauda, as it was on the featureless Zolder circuit that he had almost lost his life in 1970. On 20th May 1973, the day of the race, he seized his first real chance. He started well back and soon the no.21 BRM began to carve its way up to the front-runners in a race dominated by Stewart and Cevert's Tyrrells. With two-thirds of the race gone Niki was in fourth place, which he held

until the second-last lap when his fuel pump started to cut out and he had to dive into his pit for a quick splash n' dash. He shot back out and saw the flag in fifth place scoring his first points in F1. It was a fitting reward for all his efforts and two weeks later he was to make an even bigger impact in the Monaco Grand Prix. The teams turned up in the Principality for what is surely the most anachronistic but also the most highly mediatised race on the F1 calendar which every driver dreams of winning at least once in his life (the same goes for the supporting events). This was far from Lauda's thoughts but an exceptionally good practice lap put him on the third row of the grid so he began to think that he was on the point of finally making that

• **24 and 25**_In 1973, Niki's hunt for starting and prize money was more intense then ever. He signed with BMW and drove an Alpina coupe. In the second photo he holds his bouquet aloft after winning his class in the Spa 1000 kms with Hans Stuck as co-driver.

big impact. After his two points in Zolder his credibility would look all the better. Without passing anyone he took advantage of retirements and soon found himself in a solid third place in a car that was perfectly set up for the twists and turns of the Monaco streets. Behind him came the great Jackie Ickx in his Ferrari unable to close the gap to the young Austrian. This lasted until lap 24 when the BRM's gearbox gave up the ghost. Although satisfied with the start of the race Niki was naturally disappointed that his breakdown put a premature stop to his chances of making a big impact on F1 team managers. However, a few hundred kilometres from there in a darkened room with red shutters in the north of Italy an elderly man impressed by what he had just seen made a mental note of the young driver's name.

Louis Stanley was delighted. He had misjudged Lauda whose performance belied the rather insipid image he had projected over the previous two years. To prove it he immediately took him on as a paid driver cancelling the debts and drafts but on condition that he signed for two years. Niki was so happy with this windfall that he signed everything Stanley put in front of him. For the first time in his career he was being paid money to race! It was high time as the starting money earned in the touring cars races for BMW Alpina had all gone on settling the first payments to BRM. His Monaco performance was, as he soon discovered, a flash in the pan. Despite his efforts in the following races he qualified mid-field at best and forgettable is the most appropriate adjective to describe his race performances.

Even in D and then E configuration the P 160 chassis lacked grip and the engine needed at least another 50 bhp to worry its rivals. This, though, was all incidental to a team that was forced to scrape the bottom of the barrel to maintain the illusion that it was still worthy of its place in F1. Not until the first day of practice for the Dutch Grand Prix on the Zandvoort circuit at the end of July did the BRMs reappear at the top of the time sheets. In pouring rain typical of the North Sea climate Niki set the fastest time followed by his team-mate Clay Regazzoni. The performance was down to the Firestone tyres, which were much better adapted to the wet conditions than their rivals (the same thing was to happen in Canada at the end of the season when Lauda held the lead in the wet until the track dried out). In such cases it is

usually the driver who is credited with the performance and not the black rubber doughnuts at the car's four extremities. When he got back to the paddock after his moment of glory on Friday he learned that Ferrari wanted to see him In the dry the BRMs were back in their rightful spot (one might say) and in the race Lauda retired yet again with mechanical problems. A week later he again excelled himself thanks to his talent – helped perhaps by what had just started happening to him – and set the fifth fastest time in practice for the German Grand Prix on the 'Ring. He knew the circuit well as he had driven on it a lot when he was racing Porsche 911s and had also won the 24 Hour race in June in a BMW-Alpina Coupe with the German, Joisten, as co-driver. The 22.8 km long track was a hangover from another era and a

• **26**_ Lauda made excellent use of his Firestone tyres in the wet during the first practice for the Dutch Grand Prix setting the quickest time.

very exciting and very dangerous challenge for a driver, though if he was prepared to really push he could make a big impression. Lauda made a good start in his outdated car and was in fourth place when he went off on the first lap and injured his wrist. He withdrew from the Austrian Grand Prix and made his comeback at Monza. There he had another accident when a wheel came off sending him into the greenery in the Parabolica. By now he was now seriously demotivated as much by the fragility and unreliability of his car as by the fact that talks with Ferrari were well advanced and he had even met the old man of Maranello.

In August Clay Regazzoni, completely fed up with things at BRM, resigned for Ferrari, for whom he had driven with a fair amount of success between 1970 and 1972. The Swiss from Tessin backed Lauda's candidature. "The

old man asked me whom I wanted as team-mate. I said that Merzario was still there and he told me he didn't want him any more. As the best were by now under contract to their respective teams, I put forward Lauda's name. He was young, quick and hadn't had any problems. We also spoke about Jarier while the Italian press wanted an Italian driver. Lauda was chosen because I backed him as was confirmed by Gozzi in his recent book. (Franco Gozzi was one of Ferrari's closest collaborators from 1960 to 1995 either as press officer or salesman). There again his career would have been completely different if he hadn't come to Ferrari."

Enzo Ferrari accepted Clay's recommendation immediately as he had been very impressed by Lauda's display in Monaco when he had fended off the works Ferrari in the hands of Jackie Ickx. The Belgian had since walked out and only Arturo Merzario kept the flag flying. The Scuderia, in fact, was in a state of complete disarray because of bad technical choices concerning the design of the cars allied to internal politics. The 312 B3's monocoque was built in England by John Thompson and the car proved to be a total failure so Mauro Forghieri, banished to the production side, was called back to solve the problem. He reworked the B3 using designs from an experimental wide-bodied car called the 'snow plough' because of its very broad nose. Niki Lauda carried out his first test in the autumn in this modified B3 on the Fiorano track.

The young Austrian was completely amazed by what he saw at Ferrari. The Scuderia seemed to have unlimited funds, the backing of Fiat, the test track built the year before lined with photoelectric cells, which reproduced the main corners of several circuits, highly skilled engineers and of course the fabulous flat 12 boxer engine. After coming from a team forced to buy second-hand parts as there was not enough money for new ones he could not

understand how Ferrari had been unable to rack up championships galore. The last time the Scuderia had won the title was in 1964 with John Surtees. He now had the tools: all he had to do was to make them work.

Getting out of his contract with Stanley did not pose too many problems. He had signed for BRM for 1974 and 75 but the Englishman had not respected their agreement as he had 'forgotten' to pay Lauda his starting money and performance bonuses. In addition, Ferrari was ready to settle the loans that the young wheeler-dealer had amassed up to then. So at the end of 1973 Niki Lauda had achieved the aims he had set himself and was able to devote his time to much more interesting things than counting his debts. He admitted a few years later. *"Everything I did was completely crazy but my situation obliged me to take every possible risk. It had no influence on my driving. When you get into a car you don't think about dosh. In that era I thought no more about my debts than I did later on about the huge amounts of cash I earned."* ∎

Jean-Pierre Beltoise: "He was asked why he gave a number"

In 1973, the popular French champion was about to begin his second season with BRM when Lauda arrived. The latter had few references and Jean-Pierre tried to find out what had gone wrong for the young Austrian up to then.
"In 1972, he didn't have a very good car, a March. We saw that he was quick. Between Regga and myself there wasn't much difference. I was talking to him one day and I said: 'Niki, it's amazing how you always manage to be at the back of the grid. He answered, 'number 5807'. As it was obvious I didn't understand he continued, 'yes it's my engine number.' He had had the same engine all the time and it had almost never been changed! Let's just say that the car was a little less competitive, about 0.5s slower plus the 1.5s for engine which added up to 2 seconds a lap. And going flat out! It's interesting. He was asked why and he gave a number. I also admired him very much for taking out a big bank loan on a kind of risk capital basis. I respected his determination and his driving skills. We were all determined but to do that took a lot of gumption. I didn't want to acknowledge the fact that BRM fitted used parts to the cars. I closed my eyes. I said 'no, it's not true; they're working.' The engineers were nice guys and competent too. I felt good. I was sure it was going to work out. But BRM gambled on investing the past in the future and gradually it just fell apart. Niki analysed the situation much more realistically and pragmatically than I did."

• **27**_ With his BRM team-mate Jean-Pierre Beltoise in 1973. *(DPPI)*

(*) "300 km/h" See bibliography at the end of the book.

Chapter 6
1974
Making it in Maranello

• **29**_In 1973, Lauda and Enzo Ferrari met for the first time. Like married couples they had their ups and downs in a stormy relationship that lasted four years. It gave the Austrian his chance to make his name on the F1 scene with two World Championship titles, and for Ferrari it marked a long-awaited renaissance after a number of lean years.

When Lauda arrived at Ferrari the thought might have occurred to him that after all the lean years he was about to enjoy the fat ones. No way! A huge amount of work had to be done during the 1973-74 winter to bring Mauro Forghieri's efforts to transform the Ferrari B3 to a successful conclusion. There was no guarantee of a positive outcome as the leading Italian team had been in the doghouse for years. What Niki had going for him was his incredible will to succeed, his methodical approach and his frankness. In contrast to the vast majority of people who worked for the Scudera and did not dare contradict "Il Commendatore" the Austrian made a point of telling him just how lousy the car was especially after he tested it for the first time. The

old man, however was a much more perceptive individual than he was often given credit for and he took these criticisms as they were meant, namely, constructively. Throughout his career Lauda never beat about the bush when saying what he thought about the way the racing side was being handled and it did not always please everybody. His relationship with Enzo was a very frank one even when there were arguments, and after all these years he still has deep affection for the man he described as being "the giant author of an historic work."

Although this type of status was not current at Ferrari Niki assumed the role of no.2 driver alongside Clay Regazzoni. The Swiss was an experienced racer and the two complemented each other in the task that awaited them. *"What*

was practical," recalls Regazzoni, "was that we had a similar driving style. The car suited him as much as it did me even where the seat was concerned. He got out and I got in! We didn't have to modify the pedals, the seat. Anything."

Lauda appreciated Regga's fun-loving approach to life but even more so the man who was at the head of the team, a young Italian aristocrat, Luca Cordero di Montezemolo, called in by the Fiat president Gianni Agnelli to sort Ferrari out. He soon showed himself to be a first-class coordinator, an efficient team manager and became one of the essential cogs in the machinery that was to put Ferrari back into the winner's circle. His pragmatism and sense of judgement dovetailed with Lauda's view of how to drive the whole team forward. In the early

grands prix of the 1974 season it was evident that the B3/B4 as Forghieri christened it (contrary to what was written in the reports of the time where the term B3 was wrongly used and created confusion with the very different model of the previous year) was a big step forward in relation to the 1973 car. It was much quicker and in Buenos Aires Lauda scored his first rostrum finish with a second place followed by Regga in third, which the Swiss followed up with a second place in Interlagos where his team-mate retired. However, a lot of work still had to be done especially on the engine which suffered from poor reliability. In South Africa both drivers went out but not before Lauda showed how quick he was by setting his first pole position. He did the same at Jarama and in a race made very tricky by

• **30**_Proof of Lauda's talent as a driver came when he set his first pole in the 3rd round of the 1974 world championship on the Kyalami circuit.

P. MÉNARD

Designer: Mauro Forghieri

Engine
Make/type: Ferrari
No. of cylinders/layout: 180° V 12 (rear)
Cubic capacity: 2991.8 ccs
Bore/stroke: 80 x 49.6 mm
Compression ratio: 11.5:1
Max. power: 485 bhp
Max. revs: 12,500 rpm
Block: Alsi 9
Fuel/oil: AGIP
Plugs: Champion
Injection: Lucas
Distribution : 4 O.H.C
Number of valves per cylinder : 4
Ignition: Magnetti/Marelli
Weight: 145 kgs

Transmission
Gearbox/ no. of ratios: Ferrari (5)
Clutch: Borg & Beck

Chassis
Chassis: Load-bearing aluminium monocoque
Suspension: Double wishbone, inboard coil/ damper units (front)
Upper arm push rod, trapezoid lower link (rear)
Dampers: Koni
Wheel diameters: 13" (Front and rear)
Rim widths: 9.2" (Front) / 13.1" (Rear)
Tyres: Goodyear
Brakes: Girling

Dimensions
Wheelbase: 2518 mm
Tracks: 1625 mm (front) 1605 mm (rear)
Dry weight: 578 kgs
Fuel tank capacity: 230 litres

Used throughout the 1974 season.

the changing weather conditions, the track was wet at the start and then dried out, gave Ferrari its first victory since that of Jackie Ickx in Germany in 1972, plus fastest lap. Obviously, it was a very important win for the Austrian and it confirmed his potential as a future pretender to the world championship title. With Regazzoni's second place Ferrari's cup was full. Into third came the 1972 world champion Emerson Fittipaldi in a McLaren as he had deserted Lotus for the Woking outfit. Italy immediately adopted both drivers and seemed especially curious about the younger who came from a neighbouring country and a culture was the opposite of the peninsula's Mediterranean exuberance. To the great joy of the Tifosi Lauda spoke some Italian and communicated with them in that language. In fact, he quickly realised that it would be an advantage for him to learn the tongue so he could understand what was being said behind his back, and he set himself to this task in his usual single-minded fashion soon achieving a high degree of fluency.

The 1974 championship developed into a fight between the Ferrari drivers and Fittipaldi who was soon joined by the very quick youngster from South African, Jody Scheckter. Throughout the year the tide of battle ebbed and flowed and not until the last race was the title finally decided. Niki scored another win in Holland followed by a second place in France putting him into the world championship lead in his first season with a really competitive F1 team. After his Dutch victory many people - who had written him off in the recent past - thought that he could well win the 1974 title given his obvious class. And so once totally ignored by the media he now found himself the centre of attention with microphones being continually being thrust under his nose and interview requests pouring in: it was a change of fortune worthy of the best fairy tales! However, it was not to be.

When in the lead in the British Grand Prix on the Brands Hatch roller coaster he suddenly felt his Ferrari's handling go awry with only ten laps left in the race. His right-hand rear tyre had

• **31**_The start of the 1974 Spanish Grand Prix on a wet track. Peterson in his Lotus 76 (no.1) made a blinding getaway and led for 20 laps from Lauda (no.12) and Regazzoni (no.11). When the track began to dry the Austrian hit the front following the first round of pit stops and went on to win his first F1 grand prix.

• **32**_In 1974, the Scuderia was back on the top step of the rostrum thanks to Lauda's skill, di Montezemolo's team management, Forghieri's genius and Regga's experience.
(Alois Rottensteiner)

a slow puncture (the outdated state of the English track was to be heavily criticised by many drivers) and he tried his best to hold on to his lead but was unable to prevent first Scheckter, then Fittipaldi and Ickx from passing him. With one lap to go the red Ferrari dived into the pits with the tyre in tatters. And did not reappear as the pit lane exit was blocked with officials! Finally Lauda was classified fifth but he had lost an excellent opportunity to make a break in the championship ratings; it was almost a repeat of Monaco two months previously where he was in the lead until his alternator gave up the ghost. Little did he know that his fifth place on the Kent circuit was to be his last points scoring finish of the season.

On the Nürburgring he was again on pole but fluffed his start and was passed by Regazzoni and Scheckter in the first corner. He was hit by an attack of the red mist and in his attempts to get back in front made a beginner's mistake in the following turn, the North curve, a few hundred metres further on. He tried to get by Scheckter on the inside forgetting that as just over a kilometre had been covered the tyres were still cold and when he hit the brakes it was as if he was driving on ice. The Ferrari banged wheels with the Tyrrell and then spun off into the catch fencing. Clay scored a superb win that day which put him in the lead in the title chase. With his usual frankness Niki admitted that he

had screwed things up as a race is never won in the first corners especially on a circuit as long as the 'Ring. Next race was the Austrian Grand Prix and Lauda was anxious to make amends in front of his home crowd. A huge number of spectators turned up at the Österreichring to cheer him on as they had adopted him as a worthy successor to the late Jochen Rindt. He was again let down by his engine in the race after setting another pole. He did the same at Monza in front of stands packed with voluble hordes of Tifosi and then spent two-thirds of the race in the lead until his engine blew. This retirement more or less put paid to his world championship hopes which were finally dahed following his accident in the Canadian race. After Mosport the teams

headed on to Watkins Glen for the United States Grand Prix the last race race of the season and the championship looked set for a thrilling finale as both Regazzoni and Fittipaldi were on fifty-two points. Niki's job was to do everything possible to help his team-mate. Unfortunately, the Ferraris suffered serious suspension problems and Fittipaldi's fourth place was enough to clinch his second F1 title. For Lauda it was a very trying race as in addition to his car's unpredictable handling he was deeply affected by the death of his young fellow-countryman, Helmut Koenigg, making his grand prix debut in a Surtees which went under the guardrail on lap 10 with fatal results.

• **33**_Lauda had the British Grand Prix as good as won when a rear tyre began to deflate on the Brands Hatch circuit with the finish almost in view. It was a difficult summer for the Austrian...

• **35**_The 1974 Italian Grand Prix was his last hope on staying in the title chase. He led in the opening laps until his engine went on the blink.

• **34**_This was Niki's last year in Touring Car races in cars like the Ford Capri RS, which he shared with Jochen Mass in the Nürburgring 1000 kms (rtd). In 1975 he only raced in F1.
(DPPI)

Once he had got over his disappointment Lauda had very reason to be pleased with himself as he came fourth in the F1 Drivers' World Championship having scored two victories and had also shown that he was a potential champion. Financially he was now secure which allowed him to concentrate all his efforts on F1 and give up touring car racing in the Ford Capri RSs which he shared with Jochen Mass in particular, at the Salzburgring and the Nürburgring 1000 kms both of which ended in retirement. The Ferrari team's organisation had reached a peak of efficiency

never before attained thanks in particular to two squads of mechanics who shared the work. However, the 312B3/B4, which had showed great potential, still needed work to improve its reliability, its Achilles Heel. Recently, Mauro Forghieri told us that: *"this car was the result of necessity as it was built around an already-existing base while the 312T was a more modern car designed as a whole."* The new Ferrari, which had been worked on in secret for almost two years in Maranello by the brilliant engineer, had an additional trump card that was still shrouded in mystery. ■

Chapter 7
1975
Lauda's first
F1 title

● **37**_The chaotic start to the
1975 Spanish Grand Prix on
the Montjuich circuit led to the
elimination of both Ferraris,
which had been the quickest in
practice.
(Alois Rottensteiner)

Forghieri had resisted pressure from all sides
in Maranello to race his new car, scheduled
for 1975, in 1974. He was a perfectionist
and wanted to refine the last details so while he
accepted a brief presentation of the car before
the North American races (on 27th September at
Fiorano) he quickly removed it from under the
inquisitive noses of the press to complete its
construction. He also decided to enter two of the
old B3/B4s for the first two rounds of the world
championship to avoid any problems caused by
racing the 312T too soon. The car's first
appearance was in the Kyalami paddock.

It had refined aerodynamics, revised
suspension and a breath-taking overall shape but
the main novelty was the gearbox, which was
mounted transversally at the rear of the engine
thus minimising the polar moment of inertia. At
the time its function was a jealously guarded
secret but Forghieri told us that its advantage lay
in a small final drive, which reduced the gearbox's
speed considerably. Its performance was improved
even more by the fact that the gears were not
bathed in oil thus preventing vortexes from
forming. Its compactness allied to its location did
the rest. In 1975, only the technical crew and the
drivers were in on the secret.

In Kyalami Lauda was hopping with
impatience to start practising, as he was fully
aware of the 312T's potential. Unfortunately, he
went off on oil dropped by Emerson Fittipaldi's
McLaren's engine and the Ferrari was so badly
damaged that Montezemolo had the reserve
B3/B4 prepared. However, the mechanics worked
an all-nighter and managed to get the car ready
for next day's practice but the engine seemed
down on power and the Austrian could do no
better than fourth quickest. The problem
persisted in the race in which he finished fifth. As
there was a 2-month gap to the next round in
Spain Forghieri had all the time necessary to coax
a few more horses out of the flat 12. On 12th April
the car was entered for the International Trophy
as a shakedown test. This non-championship race
was about the only one remaining from the era
when events in which drivers and teams could
test new solutions at their leisure against top-
class opposition were all part and parcel of the
season. As the world championship calendar
became increasingly packed Goodwood, Oulton
Park, Syracuse and Solitude etc. vanished into the
mists of time. All that remained was the Race of
Champions on the Brands Hatch circuit and the
International Trophy at Silverstone. All the teams

replied present for this spring event to try out their new solutions in view of the coming European Grands Prix. Lauda scored a convincing victory in the British race reassuring everybody at Maranello about the car's speed.

The Austrian put his car on pole for the first time in the 1975 season on the tricky and dangerous Montjuich Park circuit in downtown Barcelona and alongside him on the first row was his team-mate, Regazzoni. A maiden win for the 312T looked on the cards. Both made an impeccable start but in the first hairpin after the pit straight the Austrian felt a violent clout in his Ferrari's rear, and the car went straight into the guardrail. Another impact followed and it caught fire but he managed to leap out of the cockpit. Mario Andretti, nudged by Brambilla, was the man responsible for the first bang and then Regazzoni could not avoid his team-mate hence the second. Although furious as he was an innocent victim Lauda was fortunate to emerge unscathed from the accident. Before the race the circuit's safety, or rather lack of same, had been the object of vehement criticism which was borne out at half-distance when Rolf Stommelen's Embassy-Hill flew over the guardrail after losing its rear wing killing four people and injuring several others.

Two weeks later Niki notched up another pole on the Monaco circuit and drove a perfect race to take the chequered flag. The grand prix started in the wet and he stopped at just the right moment when the track began to dry. It was a big day for Ferrari as the Scuderia's last win in the Principality went back to 1955 and Maurice Trintignant's 625. It was the beginning of Lauda's challenge for the 1975 F1 World Championship led by Fittipaldi. His victory was also down to the slick pit work of the Ferrari mechanics as his tyre change took only thirty seconds as against 1m 20s for his nearest rival and former team-mate Ronnie Peterson. It was another nine points in the bag and he won again at Zolder after another well-judged drive. The Belgian circuit was hard on brakes and tyres and although Lauda started from pole he kept out of the early battle for the lead in which Brazilian Carlos Pace in his Brabham and the 'Monza gorilla' alias Vittorio Brambilla's March ruined their tyres. He then upped the pace and went on to an unchallenged victory. Following this success people began to use expressions like "calculating tactician" and "winning machine" to describe him. In Sweden he proved his crushing superiority on a track that was reputed to be unsuitable for the Ferraris and completed his hat-trick. Next up was Zandvoort.

• **38**_After the Barcelona debacle the beautiful 312T got its revenge in Monaco: it was the first of a string of three consecutive victories for Lauda.

It looked like a fourth victory was his for the taking. He set pole, made an excellent start in the North Sea drizzle to lead the pack with consummate ease and after a couple of laps the crowd was resigned to another Lauda demonstration. Then the weather changed and everybody dived into the pits for fresh rubber. When Niki rejoined he was only three seconds behind Jarier's Shadow while in the lead was his old friend James Hunt in his Hesketh. He sliced past the Frenchman and quickly reeled in the Englishman. The crowd woke up again as it

looked like there were going to be some fireworks at last but to their surprise Niki stayed right on the Hesketh's gearbox for twenty laps trying to push Hunt into making a mistake without really launching an all-out attack. That was how they finished and when journalists questioned the Austrian after the race he explained that attempting to pass a racer like James Hunt, who was on his way to his first grand prix victory, would have been suicidal. Better to pocket six points than risk an accident. In the days that followed the public and pundits let fly! Maybe

1975 Belgian Grand Prix
Ferrari 312T

P.MÉNARD

Designer: Mauro Forghieri

Engine
Make/type: Ferrari
No. of cylinders/layout: 180° V12 (rear)
Cubic capacity: 2991.8 ccs
Bore/stroke: 80 x 49.6 mm
Compression ratio: 11.5: 1
Max. power: 495 bhp
Max. revs: 12,800 rpm
Block: Alsi 9
Fuel/oil: AGIP
Plugs: Champion
Injection: Lucas adjusted by an electric motor
Distribution : 4 OHCs
No. Of valves per cylinder : 4
Ignition: Magnetti/Marelli
Weight: 145 kgs

Transmission
Gearbox/no. of ratios: Ferrari transversal (5)
Clutch: Borg & Beck

Chassis
Type: Aluminium monocoque
Suspension: Upper rocker arm and lower wishbone (front)
Reversed lower wishbone, trailing top link (rear)
Dampers: Koni
Wheel diameters: 13" front and rear
Rim widths: 9.2" (Front) / 16.2" (Rear)
Tyres: Goodyear
Brakes: Girling

Dimensions
Wheelbase: 2518 mm
Tracks: 1510 mm front, 1530 mm rear
Fuel tank capacity: 200 litres

Used from South Africa to USA in 1975 and in Brazil and Long Beach in 1976.

Niki Lauda was the best but his wins were devoid of bravura. He drove like a kind of insipid shopkeeper and the word computer also was used to describe him.

However, if one examines his performance the figures speak for themselves. The previous year he had set 9 pole positions, a feat he would repeat in 1975. He had just racked up three successive wins and a second place, which had put him well ahead in the title chase. All in all he was a fairly rapid shopkeeper! Jackie Stewart drove like this and it was alongside him that

Lauda should be placed rather than in the Clark or Moss category. Jochen Rindt started to win when he began driving with his head rather than another part of his anatomy! Fittipaldi had done the same thing the previous year. Niki's approach did not go down well with the public who liked their champions more flamboyant, warmer and more extroverted. He was not expansive and had developed a kind of hermetic psychological shell, which did not allow entry to anything or anybody that might disturb its calm. The idea that something external could destroy what he had

• **39**_On the Zandvoort circuit Lauda decided not to risk overtaking James Hunt's Hesketh (no.24) and bag the 6 points for 2nd place, an attitude that did not go down well with certain people who castigated his calculating approach.

patiently built at such enormous risk frightened him. Years later in his memoirs he explained: *"I never stop controlling my feelings. I never give anything away; it's an idea which terrifies me. I'm too unstable, too sensitive to relinquish control. That's why I've built this system that protects me and helps me to conserve my strength."** Once a race was over Lauda did everything possible to leave the circuit, as he could not stand people who tried to jostle him and wanted to know how he'd won. He'd won and that was all there was to it. His was not the most charismatic image but it was one that was more in keeping with the increasingly professional motor racing scene. There was no longer any place for the knights of yesterday, more's the pity.

Such was his domination of the French Grand Prix that the only interest in the race was to see who would finish second. In England, a lowly eighth place was the best he could do and then on the Nürburgring he caught the public's imagination by getting round the fearsome 22.810 km Nordschleife in an amazing

6m 58.60s, becoming the first driver to dip under the 7-minute barrier. It is a record he will hold for the rest of his days as the circuit was taken off the F1 calendar in 1977. For the record, the fastest-ever lap there was set by Stefan Bellof in a Group C Porsche 956 in 6m 25.910s during the 1983 1000 kms event. This pole silenced his detractors as it showed his commitment on a circuit whose security he was starting to slate. The next day they were at it again when he finished third in a race that he could have won. He was slowed by a puncture and opted for four points. By now he was almost certain of being crowned world champion as he was so far ahead of second-placed man and winner of the German Grand Prix, Carlos Reutemann in his Brabham. However, he still needed a few more points to put the title beyond reach and like many others in such a situation he felt an increasing urge to get it over and done with after which he could go flat out. What better place to do it than in front of his home crowd on the Osterreichring where he had never had any luck since his F1 debut.

(*) "300 km/h" See bibliography at the end of the book.

In practice he put his Ferrari on pole in dry conditions but the next day in pouring rain he could do no better than scrape home sixth scoring a single point. And so to Italy where he clinched the championship in the seething Monza environment. He followed leader Regazzoni like his shadow and then when he started to feel worrying vibrations due to a blocked damper on his 312T he let Fittipaldi past as third was good enough for the title. It was a great day for Regazzoni, Ferrari and Italy, and for Niki the culmination of a marvellous year.

The programme had been crowned with success and everything had worked out as planned. Lauda, now firmly stuck with the nickname, the "computer," had proved to anybody with even a smidgen of objectivity without resorting to facile clichés that this success was the result of an enormous amount of hard work, determination and willpower. The shy, moneyless young man had had such unshakeable self-belief that he managed to overcome all the obstacles that destiny had strewn on his path and had put the most prestigious team in racing back on the road to glory. It was something that the Tifosi would never forget and a relaxed Lauda's easy win in the final round of the championship on the Watkins Glen circuit in the USA was the icing on the cake.

Personally, 1975 saw a drastic change in his private life as he was able to quit his small apartment in Salzburg thanks to his new-found wealth and had a huge house built in Hof, a nearby village. He also purchased a small plane to enable him to travel to the European Grands Prix under his own steam. He was immediately captivated by this form of transport and started taking lessons so that he could have the pleasure of flying his Cessna. Later on he saw the economic advantages of this when he started up

• **40**_On the fast Paul Ricard track Niki racked up his 4th win after those of Monaco, Zolder and Anderstorp. It looked like the title was on its way back to Maranello after Ferrari's many years in the wilderness.

• **41 et 42**_Ferrari triumphed on the Monza circuit and the Tifosi were in seventh heaven. Niki won the Drivers' title and Clay won the race helping Ferrari to victory in the Constructors' Championship.

his own aviation company. His love-life was also turned upside down when he met Marlene Kraus at a party in Curt Jurgens' house: she was the actor's mistress and Lauda fell in love with her immediately. The gutter press disclosed their relationship a few weeks later and they were married in the spring of 1976. Their two children, Lukas and Mathias, were born in 1979 and 1981 respectively. ∎

• **43**_Niki in conversation with Herbert von Karajan in a Motor Show in 1975: the famous conductor was a sports car fanatic and had a number of Porsche 911Ss and Carrera RSs plus a very rare street going Ford GT 40. *(Alois Rottensteiner)*

Clay Regazzoni:
"Niki chose his tyres himself"

The fun-loving Swiss, winner of five F1 grands prix (4 at Ferrari) and numerous endurance races tells us a story that reveals the degree of involvement of a driver like Lauda. *"One thing that left me perplexed was that when we tested together, Niki was never really quicker than me. We were always very close. Then when we arrived at a circuit for practice he was always faster. I didn't understand why and I said to myself 'shit, it's not possible that there's such a gap between us.' We had a lot of problems with the tyres, which were not radials. They were hand-made and sometimes the car pulled to the left and sometimes to the right. We played with the pressure but we never got 100% out of them. On Friday at Zandvoort in 1975 I set pole on Friday and Niki was second. Goodyear said to us that they had no new tyres for the next day and that we'd have to use the tyres destined for the grand prix.*
So on Saturday I concentrated on the car's full tank race set up. Nobody went any quicker and the grid looked like being the one decided on Friday. Then with five minutes to go my chief mechanic told me that Niki was on pole! 'How did he do that' I asked? 'They gave him four tyres and he did it.' Montezemolo then said to me that Niki went to Goodyear and demanded the tyres (I learned later on from a technician that it was thanks to Montezemolo that he was able to do this!). He examined all the rubber that Goodyear had brought to the race and there were differences in all these hand-made tyres. If you chose tyres made by the same person on the same day with the same degree of heat and humidity they were alike. If you took tyres made the day before there were small differences. Niki never had any problems because he always chose his tyres himself whereas I just trusted the technicians. It was an extra favour that he didn't really need. Thus, I was obliged to really push like hell for ten or fifteen laps to catch him and when I did I couldn't pass him, as his tyres were a big advantage. He would've had to have made a mistake but Niki never made a mistake. He was ambitious. Today Schumacher is exactly like him. It's his strength"

• **44**_Clay Regazzoni and Lauda in the latter's Cessna Golden Eagle.
(Alois Rottensteiner)

GOOD YEAR
1
Agip
NIKI LAUDA
Niki Lauda
SCHMITHELM
Speedline
SKF
arexons
CHAMPION
FERODO

Chapter 8
1976
Back from the abyss!

• **46**_The 1976 season got off to a brilliant start for Lauda and Ferrari the Austrian scoring two wins in Brazil and South Africa (photo) in the old 312T while awaiting the new T2. His rivals were gob-smacked!

Once the 1975 celebrations were over it was time to get back to work. Mauro Forghieri reckoned that the new 312T2 complying with the regulations coming into force at the Spanish Grand Prix was not yet ready and continued working on it. He decided to enter the T version for the first three grands prix on the 1976 calendar. It was still competitive and Niki won the first two races in Brazil and South Africa after which he finished second behind Clay Regazzoni in the streets of Long Beach. The Ferraris' speed and the Austrian's form boded ill for their rivals. Lauda was a bit worried by the way things were evolving in the Scuderia as his ally Luca di Montezemolo had been promoted to a management role between Ferrari and the Fiat mother company. A young man from Lancia called Daniele Audetto replaced him in the role of team manager. It did not take long for extreme tension to develop between Lauda and Audetto beginning with Regazzoni's win at Long Beach where the Austrian felt that he had favoured the Swiss. This served to reinforce his conviction that from now on he could only count upon himself. When the teams came back from the overseas campaign Niki took a few days off to look after

his new house. He borrowed a tractor from one of his neighbours to level a bank near his future swimming pool. The machine was not exactly a Ferrari and was tricky to drive. Lauda soon lost control of it and it flipped over on top of him. He was very fortunate not to be killed in the accident but the right-hand side of his body was badly bruised and he was in hellish pain from two broken ribs. What was only a small incident was soon blown up out of all proportion and had a drastic effect on Niki's career at Ferrari. The Spanish Grand Prix was coming up and he thought it would be very difficult for him to drive in it so his idyll with a certain section of the Italian population turned to the worst kind of tragi-comedy which, alas, was just a foretaste of the year that lay ahead.

The national press exaggerated the incident out of all proportion and put forward an idea that had been lurking in the dusty recesses of their minds for a long time, the Italian equivalent of finding the boy Jesus in a manger otherwise known as an Italian driver in a Ferrari! And of course Audetto jumped on the bandwagon by emphasising the presence of Regazzoni in the team, and even if he was Swiss his name had an

Italian ring to it unlike Lauda's. Enzo Ferrari himself was a bit disorientated by all these goings-on and did not throw his full weight behind the efforts to kill this storm in teacup. A journalist did a telephone interview with Lauda, who was still in hospital, to ask him what he thought of an Italian driver as his replacement. The suffering Austrian was completely gob-smacked by such a question and gave a curt reply from his hospital bed, the gist of which that all Italian drivers were good for "was a run round the church!" It was a major faux-pas but Lauda never regretted it: he had said what he thought. His status as icon went up in flames among some of the hotter-blooded members of the Italian community. With the hindsight that time confers Lauda reckons that the break with Ferrari occurred at that moment.

It was in this highly explosive atmosphere that he he met a physiotherapist and dietician called Wily Dungl. He was an odd, rather sullen individual who had looked after the national ski team with considerable success. He spent two weeks undergoing Wily's special treatment and was able to tackle the test (in every sense of the word) that Jarama represented. Against all expectations Niki drove a magnificent race on the twisty layout despite being in terrible pain and came home second behind James Hunt who had replaced Fittipaldi in the McLaren team. It was Hunt's first win of the season even though he was initially disqualified (car too wide) and then reinstated. In many ways it was also a victory for Lauda as he had proved his detractors and his team wrong – after all had he not been told to stay at home and rest by Audetto -

• **47**_Clay's win on the Long Beach circuit did nothing to help Lauda's relationship with his new team manager, Daniele Audetto, which got steadily worse as the season wore on.

Designer : Mauro Forghieri

Engine

Make/type: Ferrari
No. of cylinders/layout: 180° V 12 (rear)
Cubic capacity: 2991.8 ccs
Bore/stroke: 80 x 49.6 mm
Compression ratio: 11.5:1
Max. power: 500 bhp
Max. revs: 12,800 rpm
Block: Alsi 9
Fuel/oil: AGIP
Plugs: Champion
Injection: Lucas adjusted by an electric motor
Distribution: 4 OHCs
No. of valves per cylinder: 4
Ignition: Magnetti/Marelli
Weight: 145 kgs

Transmission

Gearbox/no. of ratios: Ferrari (5)
Clutch: Borg & Beck

Chassis

Type: Aluminium monocoque
Suspension: Upper rocker arm and lower wishbone (front)
Upper radius arm and lower wishbone (rear)
Dampers: Koni
Wheel diameters: 13" front and rear
Rim widths: 9.2" (Front) / 16.2" (Rear)
Tyres: Goodyear
Brakes: Girling

Dimensions

Wheelbase: 2560 mm
Tracks: 1405 mm (Front) / 1430 mm (Rear)
Dry weight: 575 kgs
Fuel tank capacity: 200 litres

Used from Spain to Japan.

showed tremendous courage and also let the public at large know that there was a human being behind the mask. His race was a bravura performance that made people respect him. He acknowledged that it was all down to one man, Wily Dungl who was to become Lauda's advisor concerning his physical and mental health: he taught him how to relax and let go and remained with the Austrian under the end of his career in 1985.

By Zolder he was fully fit again and won the Belgian Grand Prix as well as the next race on the Monaco circuit, a smack in the face for all those critics who had lambasted him following his tractor accident starting with Audetto with whom communication was becoming increasingly difficult. This reinforced Lauda's conviction that he was on his own and he decided to do everything in his power to win the world

championship as quickly as possible to put himself in a position of force when it came to renegotiating his contract with the "Old Man." Or whomever.

In Sweden he finished third and in France he jumped into the lead and looked set for a runaway victory until his usually reliable flat 12 engine blew after only seven laps. Niki parked his car on the trackside and watched his friend James Hunt stroll home to his second success of the year. Two weeks later they fought another memorable battle on the Brands Hatch circuit scene of the British Grand Prix. This time James again came home first on the track but was later disqualified. The FIA Court of Appeal deemed that he should not have been allowed to restart as he had not completed the full red flag lap under his own power after the race had been stopped following a first corner accident sparked off by

Regazzoni. Despite growing tension between McLaren and Ferrari the friendship between the Englishman and the Austrian remained unaffected.

The paddock was simmering with animosity when the circus arrived at the Nürburgring for the tenth round of the championship. Not only because of the problems between the English and Italians but also because of a number of comments that Lauda had made about the circuit. Built in 1927 the Eifel had always exercised tremendous fascination on spectators and drivers alike. The Nordschleife was 22,810 kms long, contained some 172 corners and had a rise and fall in altitude of 300 metres. Its blind corners surrounded by magnificent countryside, allied to capricious weather that could vary from section to section, made it unique. It was a redoubtable challenge for drivers and although a kind of romanticism grew up around it it was of the tragic kind due to a number of fatal accidents. Its length was such that in the context of modern grand prix racing's safety requirements it was completely outdated. It was mission impossible for safety services to cover its 23 odd kilometres and thus getting to the scene of an accident took much more time than elsewhere, a factor that could prove crucial in the case of serious injury. This in sum was what Lauda had said earlier on about the 'Ring when he criticised it and his words were often wrongly interpreted. The people who called him a coward and a wanker were generally those not risking their life on the track but comfortably installed in their armchairs in front of their TVs. Lauda then put the record straight: he was a professional driver and he would race at the 'Ring this year but after that he would do everything in his power to try and block the circuit's rehomologation which had been extended from 1974 to 1976 to give time for reflection. While it could be said that the Austrian's accident was not directly responsible for the track losing the F1 grand prix it certainly played a large part in the FISA's subsequent decision.

• **48**_After dominating practice Niki won the Monaco race in a canter.

• **49**_The 1976 British Grand Prix was an eventful one and its final outcome debatable. Here Lauda leads James Hunt who then passed him to take the chequered flag but was subsequently disqualified.

• **50**_Lauda's badly damaged helmet after his fiery accident on the 'Ring. The world champion had adopted this aerodynamic model made by AGV a few races before the crash in which it came off. Judging that it did not provide enough protection he went back to Bell in 1977.

A lot has been written about that 1st August 1976; and what happened on the second lap grabbed headlines worldwide. Had it been on another circuit the impact would have been much less but it was on the mythic Nürburgring. When the start was given in spitting rain under wet race conditions Niki was on the front row alongside Hunt who had set pole. He made a bad start and got caught up among the mid-field runners. He did a cautious first lap as he found the Ferrari instable on the damp track as had been the case in Saturday's practice. Then he realised it was dry in several places and pitted to put on slicks. He went back out in fourteenth place ahead of Guy Edwards who later said that he had seen the Ferrari break away on two occasions indicating that its driver had problems controlling it. As he barrelled into the fast left-hand just before Bergwerk at around 200 km/h Lauda suddenly felt the right-hand side of his car squat down and it went off into the embankment on the right-hand side. The impact was so brutal that the Ferrari cannoned off the bank and shot backwards into the middle of the road. Then hove into view a tightly packed group of three cars led by Edwards, who managed to avoid the stricken 312T2, which was then hit by Brett Lunger's Surtees and erupted in a ball of flame as petrol from the ruptured fuel tanks ignited, as well as by Harald Ertl's Hesketh. Edwards parked his undamaged car and ran back to see what could be done about getting Lauda, who had lost his helmet in the crash, out of his burning Ferrari. They struggled unsuccessfully until the arrival of Arturo Mezzario who had also stopped. The little Italian plunged into the flames, undid Lauda's harness and in a final effort pulled him out of the cockpit. Niki took a few steps and then collapsed.

He was quickly transported to the Adenau hospital and immediately rushed to Mannenheim where he lay between life and death for four days. Initially the doctors thought he was not too seriously injured. He had a broken cheek and sternum and burns on his face and hands but in fact, what was much worse was that he had inhaled toxic fumes emitted by the burning fuel, which provoked serious respiratory problems. On the evening of the third day the doctors gave him up as a hopeless case and brought in a priest to give him Extreme Unction. In his coma Niki somehow heard the priest uttering the last rites and decided that he was not going to meet the grim reaper just yet. On the morrow the doctors realised that he was still alive. Eight days later pieces of skin taken from his thigh were transplanted onto his face and skull. After this he discharged himself from hospital and went to his house in Hof to recover followed by a rest in Marlene's family's property in Ibiza. His mind soon began to function again. When could he get back behind the wheel of a car and why had he crashed? The truth will never be known but his accident was probably caused by broken right-hand suspension. However, the car was so badly damaged that it was impossible to tell. Lauda spun twice and Regazzoni thrice on the 'Ring that weekend. *"First time at the Flugplatz I spun through 360°,"* said Clay. *"The car landed pointing in the right direction so I selected first gear and set off again."* Goodyear had supplied harder tyres earlier on which had a negative effect on the dampers and the drivers had barely enough time to test them hence the difficulties in keeping the cars on the track. Whatever the case the Ferrari number one was out of action and the Scuderia soon realised just how big a loss it was for the team.

Maranello was in a state of high anxiety and took the worst possible decision, namely, to give the Austrian Grand Prix a miss. Luckily James Hunt, who had won the German event and put himself right back in the title chase, only came home fourth. Niki was appalled by his team's attitude and phoned Enzo Ferrari to ask him to get back in there and allow Regazzoni to do his best to fend off the Englishman's challenge. In the next event the Dutch Grand Prix on 29th August Clay could not prevent James from scoring another win and finished second. The Italian Grand Prix was coming up in two weeks. The world champion's decision was taken: he would return at Monza.

There was a rather strange atmosphere in the pits, which consisted of a mixture of curiosity and embarrassment as soon as practice began. The Ferrari no.1 was there, its driver too. Lauda had been given the green light by his doctors after doing thirty laps of the Fiorano test track He was not completely cured and still had dressings on his skull, which required a special modification to the interior of his crash helmet. The journalists posed awkward questions and to those who asked him if his damaged face was a handicap he answered with his usual frankness that he only needed his right foot to drive! He tried to be as much in control as possible but when it was time to take to the track it was raining. Immediately memories – speed, corners,

the rain etc.- of the Nürburgring six weeeks earlier came flooding back. Panic seized him but taking a hold on himself he reviewed the situation and decided to find his marks progressively. On Saturday he was fifth quickest better than Regazzoni and Reutemann, the new Scuderia recruit. On Sunday he drove a great race and finished fourth.

In just over a month his public image had undergone a sea change. The press praised the exploit, because that is what it was, and the public discovered that the 'computer' was also a human being. The cold and introverted champion known mainly to motor racing enthusiasts had become a super hero to the general public thanks to his brush with death; and the exceptional courage he had shown now touched even those who knew nothing about motor sport. James Hunt publicly congratulated his friend and rival for his bravery.

• **51**_Here Wily Dungl works his magic on Lauda after the accident. He looked after the Austrian until the end of the latter's career.
(Alois Rottensteiner)

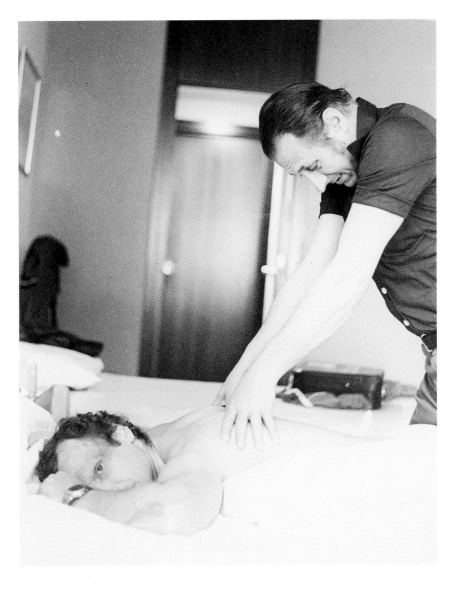

The end of the season began to take on a nightmarish quality for Lauda. His premature return had exhausted him both physically and morally and he had to call upon all his determination to continue. The Scuderia's cars were no longer competitive (which only goes to prove how much the team missed him as test driver) and he was also increasingly at loggerheads with Ferrari's policy. He was particularly irate at the Scuderia's decision to enter a third car for Reutemann (out of favour at Brabham) for Monza as it stretched the team's resources beyond their limit. The North American campaign yielded a miserable four points from the Canadian and American Grands Prix both of which were won by James Hunt. The McLaren driver was now only three points behind the man who had been favourite for the 1976 world title before Germany. Everything looked set for a thrilling show-down in the final round of the season, the Japanese Grand Prix on the Suzuka circuit. It was to be an eventful race.

It was Formula 1's first excursion to the land of the rising sun and the welcome in terms of weather anyway, was catastrophic. On race day it was bitterly cold and continuous rain pelted down from a lowering sky that touched the tips of the hills surrounding the Mount Fuji circuit. Led by Lauda the drivers thought it was sheer madness to start in such conditions and refused to get into their cars. Tension mounted as time wore on and then under increasing pressure from television and the organisers and

in the light of a probable improvement forecasted by the local weather services they gave in. Niki had already made up his mind as to what he was going to do. The race got under way with the rain still pouring down added to which was thick fog. He finished the first lap in ninth place and on the second he was floundering about in twenty-second. There would be no third time round as the no.1 Ferrari peeled off and stopped at its pit. Forghieri rushed up to see what the problem was and offered the reigning world champion an honourable way out. "When Lauda stopped he told me 'Mauro I can't drive in such conditions'. I asked him 'do you want us to say you had electrical problems?' For me it was normal to make him this kind of offer, I wanted to help." Niki refused categorically: he had taken this decision and he intended to assume it by avoiding any kind of frivolous excuse that nobody would have swallowed anyway. When Hunt crossed the line in third place to win the world championship Lauda was already in a taxi with Marlene on the way to the Haneda airport in Tokyo. Reactions to his decision were divided. There were those who castigated an attitude that they felt was unacceptable, and others who understood that he had shaken hands with death two months previously and decided that his life was more precious than any world championship. Niki was true to himself as always and did not give a damn about what people said. However, he knew that it was far from over with Ferrari. ■

Lauda's withdrawal
Error or common sense?

A lot was written and said at the time. Of course, the people who shouted the loudest were the ones who did not understand the dangers inherent in racing and what was really at stake. So it is worthwhile finding out what those who were involved in the race thought, and what it could have cost. In his memoirs Niki Lauda comes clean about his decision.

• **53**_Third lap of the 1976 Japanese Grand Prix: Lauda gets out of his car abandoning all hope of a second title. Mauro Forghieri (red cap) and Daniele Audetto (blue cap) could do nothing to change his mind.

"It was still as dangerous as before and furthermore night was falling. It went way beyond what was bearable. All I saw was rain. I was there in my car with my head hunched between my shoulders as I was afraid that someone was going to run into me at any moment. In such conditions I had no choice, I had to retire. Then a miracle happened; the rain stopped with about fifteen minutes to go but that's another story. If I could've held on until then and driving slowly to save my skin it wouldn't have been a problem to speed up in the closing laps and get a place that would've given me the title. But on that final afternoon of the 1976 season I had neither the strength nor the patience."

Mauro Forghieri said that, "psychologically Lauda was finished. He'd had his terrible accident on the Nürburgring in the summer after which he hovered between life and death for a few days. And I could understand what was happening in the mind of somebody who'd been through such an ordeal. But I have to tell you that I was personally against his comeback in the Italian Grand Prix. I thought it was not in his interest to allow him to do that. I was only the technical director, not the team manager much less Enzo Ferrari. Lauda came back to racing when he still hadn't solved the psychological problems associated with his crash."

Clay Regazzoni's reply is fairly typical of his hot-blooded temperament. "No driver can stay in bed for six months! If he wants to he has to be able to race. Otherwise it's a downer. It's obvious. After an accident all a driver wants to do is get back in the car. We've seen drivers who raced with their leg in plaster. Niki wasn't the prettiest sight at Monza: he was a bit scorched but apart from that he was psychologically quite strong. Above all it was the team which made a lot of mistakes. It was dramatic for Ferrari. We didn't go to Austria, which was a blunder as we could've scored some points there. And then when Niki stopped in Japan everybody left, Forghieri, the lot. But I was still racing! And when I came to put on slicks it was too late. The other teams had called in their drivers much sooner. I was in fifth place and I should have come in about twenty laps earlier when they realised that the rain tyres were no longer competitive. But at that moment there was nobody managing the Ferrari team."

It is worth remembering that Clay paid a high price for his love of racing. He crashed his Ensign in 1980 at Long Beach and has remained paralysed from the waist down ever since. However, he still competes in historic events in cars with paddles mounted on the steering wheel.

Another driver who knows all about the risks encountered when one gets behind the steering wheel gives us his opinion. Jean-Pierre Beltoise could have died in his René-Bonnet in an horrific accident on the Reims circuit during the 1964 12-Hour race had he not been saved by a marshal. He came out of it without the full use of his left arm and a particularly sensitive approach to safety while remaining a true racer. He gives us his own opinion with his usual frankness. *" Personally speaking I thought that the Spa circuit was too dangerous in 1974 but I didn't refuse to drive. I went to see my boss Jean-Luc Lagadère and I said to him, 'I don't really want to go there so if you can find someone to replace me, do it.' But if he had said to me, 'Jean-Pierre I want you to go there,' I'd have obeyed. I was under orders and I'd have done my very best but I wouldn't have stopped. When a driver has nothing to gain and he thinks the situation is dangerous and refuses to start I approve. On the other hand when you've built up a lead over fifteen races in the world championship and all you've got to do is drive steadily, it's unforgivable. Don't misunderstand me. What I've said is the opinion of a balanced individual who's had to fight to get where he is – and maybe Lauda's had a tougher time than me. As you've seen I admire his way of doing things but that day he blew it. And a great driver never blows it. All he has to do is to be careful and measure the distance between him and the guy in front and drive quickly enough not to be hit from behind and wait for things to sort themselves out. At the time I was very hard on him; less now as I've learned that he's analysed the situation in the same way and that he was incapable of taking the psychological pressure."*

Chapter 9
1977
Trial of strength

• **55**_Niki Lauda began the 1977 season in an interim version of the T2 as seen here in Argentina. He had been demoted to the role of no.2 driver which only served to reinforce his motivation.

When Lauda came back to Maranello after the 1976 Japanese Grand Prix he realised that what Ferrari reproached him was not so much his decision to throw in the towel at Mount Fuji but his return at Monza. For 'Il Commendatore' Hunt's world championship title would have had much less value if the Austrian had stayed in bed! And to cap it all he offered him a job as technical or sporting director. Niki saw red and harangued the old man about his fighting spirit, which was just the opposite of this petty attitude. He also insisted on his rights as laid down in the 1977 contract that had been signed by both parties in May 1976. Ferrari had no comeback to that and was obliged to retract. However, he stated that Carlos Reutemann would be no.1 driver for the 1977 season as Regazzoni had been fired. Also out was Audetto replaced by the frail Roberto Nosetto who drove Lauda crazy. And so once again he was alone given the overall suspicion with which the team regarded him. He was both excited and angry at the challenge that this represented and was determined to use his power when the right moment arose.

After the two South American races that opened the 1977 championship Lauda's best was a hard-earned third place on the Interlagos circuit while Reutemann finished third in Argentina and won in Brazil to take the championship lead. Thus, Carlos had priority concerning the latest technical developments such as a new wing in Brazil. This did nothing to change Niki's attitude to his team-mate: he couldn't stand him right from the start and as the year wore on this feeling kept growing in intensity. As to who was number one or two he drew on his considerable experience and his skills to show that on the track anyway this situation was irrelevant.

Despite Reutemann's Brazilian win Lauda was sure that the latest iteration of the 312T2 suffered from a serious aerodynamic problem. He persuaded Ferrari to organise a test session under his control before the South African Grand Prix, and managed to find a satisfactory compromise with Forghieri's help. While the collaboration between the Austrian and the Italian was very successful technically speaking it became a lot stormier that season because of a confrontation between two men both of whom had very fixed ideas. However, fruit of their collaboration came in Kyalami where Niki won his first race of the 1977 season, which was a

personal triumph as he had to call upon all his race craft and experience. He was second behind James Hunt after the start and then went into the lead on lap 7. The Ferrari was going like a train on the long straight and handling like a dream in the twisty sections of the magnificent South African track. Then on lap 22 out of the 78 scheduled he came over the blind hump on the straight in front of the pits. In a fraction of a second he saw debris on the track and could not avoid running over what looked like a rollbar (it belonged to the Shadow driven by the unfortunate Tom Pryce who had been killed a few seconds earlier by an extinguisher carried by a marshal who was hit by the Welshman's car when crossing the track). The rollbar lodged itself in the Ferrari's left-hand water tank after having modified the front wing's angle of attack. Niki immediately realised there was a problem as he felt his car going into severe understeer, which slowed him considerably. In his mirrors now loomed the threat of Jody Scheckter's Wolf. He had to change tactics. If he was able to keep the South African at bay in the twisty bits then he could count on the extra power of his Ferrari (around 500 bhp as against the Cosworth's 470) on the straight to give himself some breathing space. And so each lap he went into the corners as delicately as possible to avoid going straight

Designer: Mauro Forghieri

Engine

Make/type: Ferrari
No. of cylinders/layout: 180° V 12 (rear)
Cubic capacity: 2991.8 ccs
Bore/stroke: 80 x 46.9 mm
Compression ratio: 11.5:1
Max. power: 500 bhp
Max. revs: 12,800 rpm
Block: Alsi 9
Fuel/oil: AGIP
Plugs: Champion
Injection: Lucas adjusted by electric motor
Distribution: 4 OHCs
No. of valves per cylinder: 4
Ignition: Magnetti/Marelli
Weight: 145 kgs

Transmission

Gearbox/no. of ratios: Ferrari (5)
Clutch: Borg & Beck

Chassis

Type: Aluminium monocoque
Suspension: Upper rocker arm and lower wishbone (front)
Upper torsion bar and lower wishbone (rear)
Dampers: Koni
Wheel diameters: 13" front and rear
Rim widths: 9.2" (Front) / 16.2" (Rear)
Tyres: Goodyear
Brakes: Girling

Dimensions

Wheelbase: 2560 mm
Tracks: 1405 mm (Front) / 1430 mm (Rear)
Dry weight: 575 kgs
Fuel tank capacity: 200 litres

Used throughout the season.

on and then when he was on the straight it was pedal to metal all the way. Suddenly a red warning light came on: oil! Its level had gone down and the car ran the risk of overheating. If he lifted off too much then Scheckter would pass him and so he had to juggle with all these parameters simultaneously while praying that the engine would not blow up as the water level was falling too – and for good reason! It was fairly hot under the red helmet for the final twenty laps and then deliverance! It was his first victory since his accident, his withdrawal and his demotion to the rank of coolie! While the conditions did not lend themselves to rejoicing after Pryce's death, Niki felt pretty happy inside especially as Retutemann came home in an anonymous eighth place.

Once the celebrations were over the team was forced to acknowledge that the 1977 version of the Ferrari 312T2 was not the dominant weapon that the 1975 312T and the T2 of the first half of the 1976 season, had been. In addition, the Scuderia was up against a new rival, Mario Andretti's ground effect Lotus 78 designed by Colin Chapman in which the American scored two telling victories at Long Beach and Jarama. In California Niki finished second but in Spain he was the victim of horrific rib pains, a sequel of his Nürburgring accident, which almost cut him in two during practice. He had to be rushed to Austria to see Wily Dungl which did nothing to dampen the animosity towards him at Ferrari. Indeed Enzo publicly slammed his driver's fragility in the press!

• **57**_Niki's team-mate was Argentinean Carlos Reutemann. To say the two men disliked each other would be an understatement! Lauda did a quiet demolition job on him and won the championship.
(Alois Rottensteiner)

Mauro Forghieri:
"He was the ideal driver in the perspective of the world championship."

Mauro Forghieri joined Ferrari in 1959 and was technical director from 1962 to 1986 (with the odd break) racking up an incredible string of results in F1 and Endurance. He worked with Lauda for four years and although it was not always plain sailing between them, it was a very successful partnership.

"When Niki arrived at Ferrari he was a young driver without much experience. He was ready to give his all. We often worked from 8 a.m until the evening when it was too dark to test. Clay Regazzoni had more experience than him at the start but bit-by-bit Niki became a superb test driver. He was very quick both on the track and off as his intelligence enabled him to assimilate information very rapidly. He integrated himself into the Ferrari team almost immediately and learned enough Italian to be able to communicate. This helped him to make himself understood by the mechanics. He and I spoke English mostly. Sometimes we had three-sided conversations with the guys from Goodyear who only spoke English. He learned an enormous amount at the end of 1973 and in 1974. At the beginning at least the ambience at Ferrari was ideal for him. For me Lauda and Chris Amon were the two best test drivers the Scuderia ever had the difference being that Lauda unlike Amon functioned perfectly within the team. I knew that when I gave him a car that was working well he'd win. He was exactly the right person in the perspective of the world championship. He calculated everything, and knew exactly which path to follow. He was one of the drivers with whom I had the best working relationship. Unfortunately, he changed after two years. Above all it was his plane that modified his way of seeing things. He became less open. He had his Cessna, which enabled him to go to Ibiza where he stayed for long periods, and naturally our work as a team suffered. When I changed the working methods in 1973 I used to write the working programmes month by month. Their precision depended on what was happening, and not just in the race. And that was the time when Lauda arrived and then wanted to get away as soon as possible. We fought about this, especially in 1977. At one moment it was open war between us. I think that he left because of money. He wasn't earning as much at Ferrari as he could have got with other teams."

Grosser Preis
von Hockenheim-Ring
Deutschland

• **59**_Lauda scored a telling victory in the title chase in the German Grand Prix on the Hockenheim circuit. Sharing the rostrum with him are Jody Scheckter (2ⁿᵈ) and Hans Stuck (3ʳᵈ).

Wily again worked his magic and Lauda strung together a set of results that he felt was in keeping with his car's potential. He racked up three second places in Monaco, Zolder and Silverstone enabling him to hang on to the championship lead. Once again his critics emerged from the swamp like an army of croaking frogs, "Lauda only does what's necessary and has no flair." The press and the public began to root for the more flamboyant Andretti and battling James Hunt, who was back in contention, rather than for Lauda the computer. But the latter pair tended to race in ON-OFF mode. The Austrian upped the ante a notch when he won the German Grand Prix on the featureless Hockenheim circuit where power was all that mattered an area in which Ferrari had an advantage over Cosworth. In Austria he added yet another second place to his tally followed by victory in Holland, which put him in an ideal situation as the Italian Grand Prix, the last European round of the championship, approached. It was also time for Niki to settle his scores.

Bernie Ecclestone, the powerful boss of the FOCA (Formula One Constructors' Association)

and owner of Brabham, had figured out exactly how Niki felt about Ferrari. He asked him to come to Chessington where the team was based to see Gordon Murray's latest creation, the BT46 powered by a flat 12 Alfa Romeo engine. Lauda thought it was quite simply fantastic with all its on-board electronics and original surface cooling. Once the contract had been sorted out Bernie and Niki shook hands. The Austrian would be John Watson's team-mate in 1978 at Brabham and he quickly handed in his resignation to Ferrari. The news hit the headlines a few days before the Italian Grand Prix which promised a Monza cauldron hotter than ever.

On the morning of first practice Niki Lauda and the Ferrari team received a mixed reception. For some of the Tifosi the team would not recover from the loss of the world champion and they made their feelings know to the team management in no uncertain terms. Others were much more worked up and insulted Lauda who had again become the "Austrian." Enzo Ferrari too unleashed his venom to the press concerning "that Judas who sold himself to the rivals (Alfa Romeo of course) for thirty kilos of salami;' an allusion to the personal contract

Lauda had signed with the huge dairy company, Parmalat, which would become the Brabham title sponsor for nigh on ten years. In this overheated atmosphere Niki again finished second behind Mario Andretti's black and gold Lotus and prepared to set off for the USA to score the one point he needed to clinch his second F1 title.

The United States Grand Prix was held in pouring rain in very similar conditions to the previous year in Japan. This time Lauda did not withdraw not that he had changed his mind about what he had denounced in the past but applied the tactics he should have followed on the Mount Fuji circuit. The main difference was that he was psychologically strong enough to stay on the track and score the point that he needed. He came home fourth after a rather lacklustre race and was crowned world champion for the second time.

There are two ways of evaluating his title – as many observers were at pains to point out. The first was that it was a just reward for a driver who showed his true talent only on rare occasions and privileged consistency over brio as he saw the flag on more occasions than his

rivals. Or that he was alone and had to fight against his team, his team-mate and Italy in a car that was basically no longer capable of competing with the opposition except on rare occasions. He had proved to the world at large that his accident had in no way diminished his talent, rather it had changed the way he tackled racing.

His career with Ferrari ended earlier than scheduled. He cried off the Canadian race on the morning of first practice as he was suffered from a stomach infection (or at least that was the official version). He then refused to race in Japan in protest after Ferrari fired his personal mechanic, Ermano Cuoghi, as the latter had somewhat rashly announced that he would be following Lauda to Brabham. Both sets of spectators were not very happy with his decision, to say the least! To sum up it has to be said that Ferrari and Lauda gave each other a lot more than this rather nasty end to their relationship let on. The former put the Austrian on the world stage and he in turn brought the Italian team the success that it had been chasing for many years. Mutual passion often ends in bitter separation, though! ■

• **60**_He finished 4th in the USA Grand Prix on the Watkins Glen circuit to win his second F1 Drivers' title. He was allowed to join the winner, James Hunt (complete with fag and beer!) on the rostrum. It was sweet revenge for the Austrian.

Chapter 10
1978
Deception lies behind the fan

• **62**_The Brabham team
began the season with
outdated BT45Cs in which
Lauda did his best to rack up a
few points.

etween the moment that Niki Lauda saw
the future BT46 at the Brabham factory in
Chessington and his first test in the car
Gordon Murray had come to the conclusion that
his surface cooling system would never work. It
was his most serious setback since taking on the
job of technical director at Brabham in 1971.
And so Watson and Lauda had to start the
season in a pair of BT45Cs which were hardly the
most competitive cars around. Nevertheless in
keeping with his reputation Niki got the best out
of the Brabham and finished second in Argentina
and then third in Brazil.

He was happy to be in the English team.
Compared with the political intrigue that
poisoned Ferrari Brabham was a small outfit and
it was easy to talk to Murray and Ecclestone. The
Chessington squad was much more vulnerable
than its bigger rivals to major setbacks because

it was so small. Ecclestone spent the greater part
of his time in his role as Formula 1's big cheese
rather than looking after his team, something
that Niki would soon regret. Brabham's other
major problem was the Alfa Romeo engine. On
paper it was the most powerful of the lot with
its 520 bhp but it was as fragile as spun glass
due mainly to overheating problems, which
Murray initially thought he had solved with his
surface cooling technology. However, the
versatile engineer had already started designing
another system but it would take time to
develop it. In the meantime the drivers had to
put up with the caprices of the engine penned
by Carlo Chiti, the head of Auto Delta, which
looked after Alfa Romeo's competitions
programme.

In practice things usually went pretty well
and the BT46s proved very quick. For example,

Designer: Gordon Murray

Engine

Engine/type: Alfa Romeo 115-12
No. of cylinders/layout: Flat 12 (rear)
Cubic capacity: 2993 ccs
Bore/stroke: 78.5 x 51.5 mm
Compression t ratio: 11.5:1
Max. power: 520 bhp
Max. revs: 12,000 rpm
Block: Aluminium
Fuel/oil: AGIP
Plugs: Champion
Injection: Lucas/SPICA
Distribution: 4 O.H.Cs
No. of valves per cylinder: 4
Ignition: Marelli Dinoplex
Weight: 170 kgs

Transmission

Gearbox/ no. of ratios: Brabham Alfa (6)
Clutch: Borg & Beck

Chassis

Type: Aluminium monocoque
Suspension: Double wishbone, semi-suspended springs (front
2x2 lower arms, 2x1 upper arms, 2x2 unsuspended push rods (rear)
Dampers: Koni
Wheel diameters: 13" front and rear
Rim widths: 10" (Front) / 18" (Rear)
Tyres: Goodyear
Brakes: Girling/Dunlop

Dimensions

Wheelbase: 2499 mm
Tracks: 1448 mm (Front) / 1524 mm (Rear)
Dry weight: 611 kgs
Fuel tank capacity: 209 litres

Raced in Argentina and Brazil.

Niki secured pole position in South Africa but in the races themselves the engine suffered from disastrous reliability and forced the Austrian to change his driving style. To try and match the pace-setting ground-effect Lotus 79s in the hands of Andretti and Peterson he was obliged to drive in attack mode all the time and abandon his usual prudent approach. This delighted a large number of pundits who had pigeonholed him the previous year. In Monaco for example, he was victim of a puncture when in second place behind Depailler's Tyrrell. He pitted and then made an astonishing comeback from sixth to second position. His performance earned him the admiration of many of his detractors. The car's doubtful reliability hindered the Austrian's consistent approach to racing but he was still in contention for the title when the circus arrived in Sweden.

Gordon Murray had just come up with an inspired solution through a clever interpretation of the regulations. He analysed the recurring overheating problems in the Alfa engine which he decided to cool by fitting a big radiator horizontally above the cam covers. Additional cooling was provided by a large fan mounted under the rear wing behind the block. Murray told us recently that the spirit of the law was respected as the main purpose of the fan was to cool the engine. The fact that it glued the Brabham to the road like a leech thanks to a system of skirts was only secondary! In fact, the ingenious South African engineer had found a way to counter the ground effect created by Colin Chapman and his Lotus 78 (79 in 1978). Of course at the time he could not say it openly. He gave the following figures: 57% for cooling purposes and 43% for the aerodynamic effect.

• **63**_The new BT46 had a more fluid shape and was quicker than the 45C as Lauda proved by putting it on pole on its Kyalami debut. Unfortunately, the flat 12 Alfa was still as capricious as ever and in the race it seized as it was to do on numerous other occasions.

• **64**_Niki drove one of the best races of his career in Monaco. Without his puncture he would have won the grand prix, and he proved it was possible to overtake in the streets of the Principality as he stormed from 6th to 2nd place just behind Depailler's winning Tyrrell after his wheel change.

These were later corroborated by the CSI, the sporting arm of the FIA. It was the 43% that posed problems for Brabham's rivals. *"Nobody could beat us,"* Murray remembers with a smile. *"The guys could've driven this car on the ceiling!"* And in Sweden the car beat its rivals into a cocked hat.

Lauda and Watson were well aware of the potential of such a device and the havoc it could play with the other teams so they did everything to avoid getting pole, which fell to Andretti in the Lotus 79. In the race itself Niki followed the American like his shadow and looked as if he was playing cat and mouse with him. When the Lotus

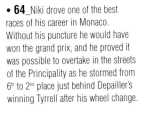

hit some oil spilled by another car its wheels began to spin on the greasy track and the Brahham BT46B fan car went by as if it were standing still! Andretti still hasn't got over it. Lauda went on to score an overwhelmingly easy victory. What Murray had predicted was coming true. The car was examined by the CSI who could

only admit the primary function of the fan was for cooling the engine and the win was officialised. Then came the backlash that Lauda and Murray were to regret and it was all down to Ecclestone's highly political involvement in the F1 regulations. The constructors put pressure on him stating that if he did not withdraw this diabolical

• **65**_Ferrari and Brabham fight for the lead as they rush into the first corner on the Long Beach circuit. Watson (no.2) tries to go through on the inside of Reutemann (no.11) with Lauda (no.1) and Villeneuve (no.12) also monstering the Argentinean. Once again Lauda was let down by his engine.

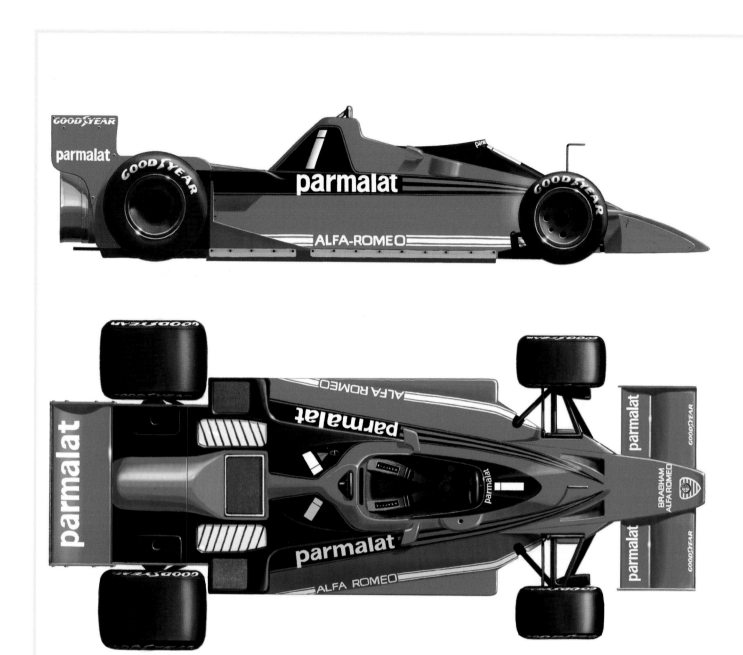

machine they would not back him in the FOCA. Their main argument was that the fan threw up stones, which were very dangerous for the cars following. Thus, the BT46B was not banned by the authorities as was said in the past but was withdrawn voluntarily by Ecclestone who preferred to lose the championship rather than control of his budding empire!

Niki commented recently on this unique F1 machine. *"When I tested the BT46 fan car for the first time on the Brands Hatch circuit it was not all that well balanced and I really had to learn to*

drive it. It suffered from tremendous understeer on the exit from corners and, whereas normally in such a case you lift off I realised that you had to accelerate hard as the fan driven by the engine began to revolve even quicker and glued the car to the track. Then when we raced in Sweden we'd found the right balance; everything was working properly and I scored an easy victory. It had become an unbelievable weapon but it had no future as if we'd been let develop it it'd have killed everybody. It was a dangerous car!"

1978 Swedish Grand Prix
Brabham BT46B-Alfa Romeo

P. MÉNARD

Brabham BT46-Alfa Romeo

Designer: Gordon Murray

Engine
Make/type: Alfa Romeo 115-12
No. of cylinders/location: Flat 12 (rear)
Cubic capacity: 2993 ccs
Bore/stroke: 78.5 x 51.5 mm
Compression ratio: 11.5:1
Max. power: 520 bhp
Max. revs: 12,000 rpm
Block: Aluminium
Fuel/oil: AGIP
Plugs: Champion
Injection: Lucas/SPICA
Distribution: 4 OHCs
No. of valves per cylinder: 4
Ignition: Marelli Dinoplex
Weight: 170 kgs

Transmission
Gearbox/no. of ratios: Brabham Alfa (5/6)
Clutch: Borg & Beck

Chassis
Type: Aluminium monocoque
Suspension: Double wishbone, suspended springs, front
Parallel links, rear
Dampers: Koni
Wheel diameters: 13" front and rear
Rim widths: 10" (Front) /18" (Rear)
Tyres: Goodyear
Brakes: Girling/Dunlop

Dimensions
Wheelbase: 2590 mm
Tracks: 1549 mm front and rear
Dry weight: 599 kgs
Fuel tank capacity: 205 litres

Raced from South Africa to Canada (Sweden excepted).

Brabham BT46B-Alfa Romeo
Technical characteristics identical to the BT46 except:

Chassis
Brakes: Girling

Dimensions
Tracks: 1626 front and rear
Dry weight: 629 kgs

Raced in Sweden.

• **66**_Bernie Ecclestone and Niki Lauda complimented each other in certain ways but their partnership was not crowned with success.

• **67**_The infamous fan car. The enormous ventilator placed under the rear wing of the BT46B provoked a wave of discontent in Sweden. Lauda's victory, though, was homologated. The infamous fan car. The enormous ventilator placed under the rear wing of the BT46B provoked a wave of discontent in Sweden. Lauda's victory, though, was homologated.
(Alois Rottensteiner)

Once the BT46B had been shelved the team fell back on the BT46. Lauda was once again faced with a view of the Lotus's rump and the sound of blown engines ringing in his ears. He almost won the British Grand Prix on the Brands Hatch circuit once both Lotuses had retired. He was in the lead just ahead of Reutemann and when they came up to lap Bruno Giacomelli's Alfa in Clearways he tried to go round him on the outside while Carlos slipped through on the inside of the corner. He did his best to repass the Argentinean but to no avail and finished on the tail of his 'friend' cursing the Italian's bad driving.

He did score another victory that year but in tragic circumstances in the Italian Grand Prix on the Monza circuit. There a huge pile up on the opening lap in the place where the cars left the wide open start and finish area and funnelled into the zone in which the road leading down to the first chicane narrowed. Several cars were too badly damaged to take the restart and Brambilla and Peterson were badly injured. The Italian suffered concussion from which he recovered but the Swede died the following morning due to an embolism caused by bone marrow seeping into his bloodstream. The restart was also chaotic as

the cars were held for far too long under the red light and Villeneuve imitated by Andretti began to inch forward before the green came on. When it was finally given the two cars were already under way and although Mario finished first followed by the young Canadian they were both given a 1-minute penalty for jumping the start so victory went to Lauda in third place. The Austrian publicly showed his disdain for the organisers by jumping into his plane immediately after the finish leaving it up to Watson to go and collect his cup, which, in any case was of no importance for him.

His season ended with two retirements in North America and Canada where he met the driver who was to be his team-mate in 1979, Nelson Piquet (real name Stotmayor), the recently crowned 1978 British F3 Championship who looked a better bet than Watson. He drove the third BT46 on the Notre Dame circuit in Montreal finishing eleventh. Lauda still had faith in Gordon Murray despite the repeated mechanical failures which had prevented him from defending his crown and reckoned that he would find a solution to the problems. Things would be different in 1979 as a full wing car was under construction. ■

• **68**_Niki scored a joyless victory in the tragic 1978 Italian Grand Prix.

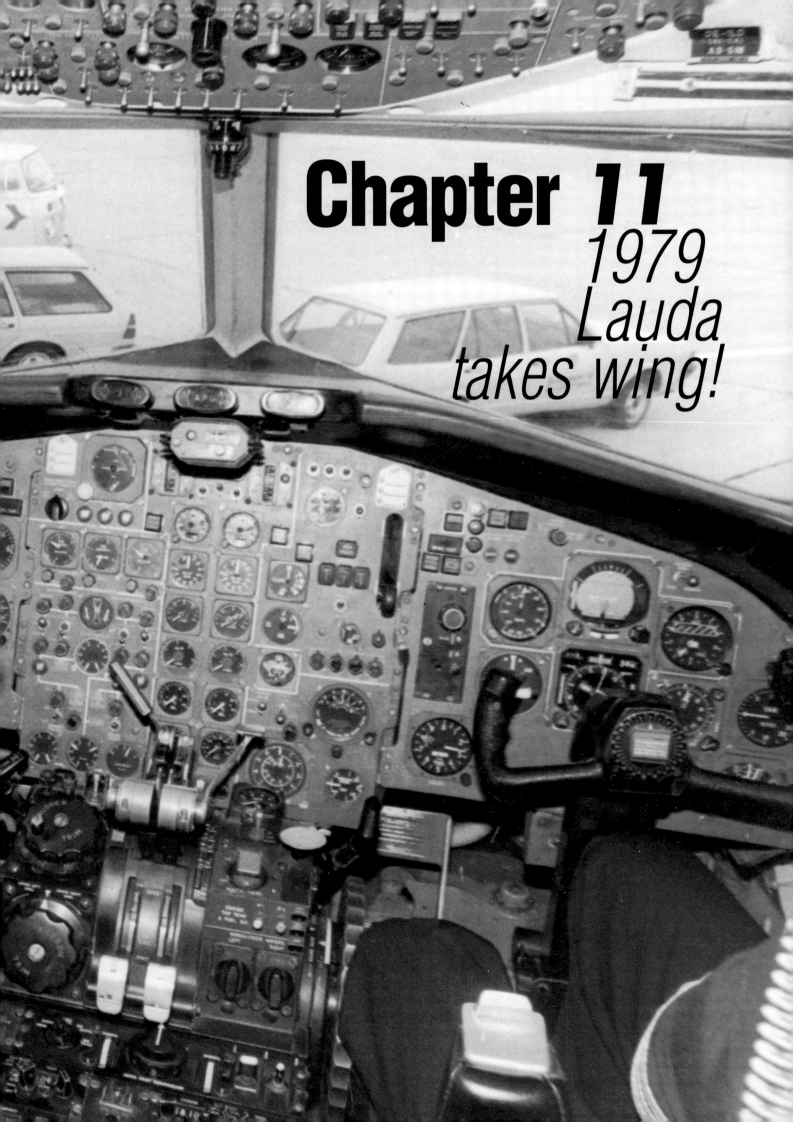

Chapter 11
1979 Lauda takes wing!

• **70**_Lauda relishes his new role as managing director of his eponymous airline in the company of his wife, Marlene, with one of his planes in the background. As his company began to take up more and more of his time he turned away from racing in 1979.

Aged twenty-nine Niki Lauda was a very happy man. He had won the F1 World Championhsip twice and had become one of the great names in the history of racing as well as a multi-millionaire due to his huge income from contracts that his employers had been persuaded (or were resigned!) to signing with him. His publicity value was enormous as witnessed by the red Parmalat cap that he wore everytime he poked his nose out of doors (he managed to earn money from it up to 2002). Even when dressed to the nines he still kept his cap firmly jammed on his balding pate whose hair had been burned away in his fiery accident. Anyway he was much

more interested in filling his piggybank that cutting a dash in society. Even if Lauda with a dose of self-derision has described himself as a Scrooge going over his accounts with a fine toothcomb he knew when to spend his dosh, especially where aircraft were concerned. After obtaining his pilot's licence in 1976 he subsequently passed more exams until he was allowed to fly his own jets. In 1978, an airline concession came up for sale and backed by the Erste Österreichische Sparkasse that had also helped him on his F2 debut in 1971, he set up his own company, Lauda Air, whose role – for the moment anyway – was to exploit small niche

Designer: Gordon Murray

Engine

Make/type: Alfa Romeo 1260
Number of cylinders/layout: V12 (rear)
Cubic capacity: 2991 ccs
Bore/stroke: 78.5 x 51.5 mm
Compression ratio: 12:1
Max. power: 525 bhp
Max. revs: 12,300
Block: Aluminium
Fuel/oil: AGIP
Plugs: Champion
Ignition: Lucas
Distribution: 4 O.H.Cs
No. of valves per cylinder : 4
Ignition: Magnetti/Marelli
Weight: 170 kgs

Transmission

Gearbox/no. of ratios: Brabham Alfa (5/6)
Clutch: Borg & Beck

Chassis

Type: Aluminium monocoque
Suspension: Pull rod double wishbone all round,
 inboard-mounted coil/spring dampers
Dampers: Koni
Wheel diameters: 13" front and rear
Rim widths: 10" (Front) / 18" (Rear)
Tyres: Goodyear
Brakes. Girling/Dunlop

Dimensions

Wheelbase: 2743 mm
Tracks: 1702 mm (Front) / 1626 mm (Rear)
Dry weight: 595 kgs
Fuel tank capacity: 200 litres

Raced all season.

markets abandoned by Austrian Airlines. It was to be an important decision. His other aim in 1979 was to win back his title and hopefully the ground effect Brabham BT48 was the right weapon to beat the Lotus 79s. It looked the part with its carbon fibre panels either side of the cockpit and the bulky flat 12 Alfa Romeo engine was replaced by a V12, which improved the airflow through the pontoons. The engine, built in only three months, was the direct cause of a nightmare season for the Brabham team. Lauda and Piquet started twenty-eight times and scored points on only three occasions! Niki's best was sixth on the Kyalami circuit and fourth at Monza. His only victory came in the short non-championship grand prix on the Imola circuit. For someone who wanted to reconquer his title it was devastating. None of the Alfa Romeo blocks was the same. The engine speed varied from one to the other. A certain number drowned in a bath of oil while others were let down by their accessories. Ecclestone was so fed up by mid-season that he decided to break with the Italian company and come back to Cosworth. Murray finished the BT49-Cosworth programme in record time and the car was entered for the final races of the season in preparation for 1980. To fine tune the car properly Ecclestone needed Niki's talents as test driver.

• **71**_The new BT48 made its debut in Argentina with a very low line rear wing. It generated less downforce and upset the car's handling so it was moved to a more conventional position.

Lauda had begun the season highly motivated but as the year wore on he became increasingly convinced that he was wasting his time. If Ecclestone wanted him then he would have to pay the price. And that was two million dollars for 1980 an amount that no racing driver had ever asked for before! Bernie was gob-smacked by such a request and told the Austrian that the Alfa engines were not the only things that had overheated! Discussions ground to a brutal halt. They restarted a few months later as the season neared its end. The Brabham boss was not very happy about starting the new Cosworth programme with the inexperienced Piquet and asked Lauda to make him an offer. The later was increasingly detached from what was going on around him and did not budge concerning his price. Ecclestone gave in and the contract was signed for 1980.

Once this had been done Lauda discovered the hollowness of it all. He realised that what had excited him was not the fact of obtaining two million dollars but besting the Machiavellian Ecclestone. And once he had done this he saw that it was all vanity. He no longer wanted, in his own words, "to drive round in circles like an idiot." His airline which was just taking off was not helped by the aggressive attitude of Austrian Airlines which had no intention of letting a mere racing driver invade its air space. Henceforth, Lauda had to invest an enormous amount of time and energy in this new battle thus he had little time left for other activities. On the morning of first practice for the Canadian Grand Prix an unenthusiastic double world champion turned up on the Montreal circuit where his brand new BT49-Cosworth awaited him.

• **72**_Lauda (no.5) scored his only points finishes in South Africa (here) and Italy towards the end of the season.

• 73_Niki Lauda, Herbie Blash, Gordon Murray and Bernie Ecclestone huddled over data from the BT48-Alfa Romeo. They could read them upside down or inside out: the result was the same: disaster.

He did a few slow laps and came into his pit. While the mechanics made detail adjustments demanded by Lauda the latter went to see Bernie. He told him that he had had enough and asked to be released from his contract. The latter acceded to his request without hesitation and wished him the best of luck in his new venture. It just so happened that young Argentinean, Ricardo Zunino, was in the pits (!) and wearing the famous red helmet with the Parmalat logo that had belonged to the Austrian he was immediately popped into the no.5 Brabham. Niki packed his bag and without even a goodbye to the team left the track, returned to his hotel and then went to the airport. There he took a direct flight to Los Angeles where his next port of call was the McDonald aircraft factory.

Thus Niki Lauda's racing career ended in an abrupt and disconcerting fashion. Naturally it raised a host of questions. For many it was typical of the 'couldn't give a damn' attitude of a driver who once again did not meet his obligations to his public, and above all to his mechanics who had spent the whole night getting the cars ready. Even though it was a well known fact that he took unilateral decisions on which there no going back and that others just had to live with, it was difficult not to think that he lacked class at the very moment when it was time to appraise his brief but exceptional career. But Lauda did not care about that either: all that mattered to him was his future which henceforth was some 30,000 feet above what he already felt were petty considerations belonging to the past. A parallel could be drawn with the exemplary attitude of the 1979 F1 world champion, Jody Scheckter, when he decided to hang up his helmet at the end of the 1980 season that had been even more disastrous than Lauda's. Jody carried on right up to the bitter end finishing his last grand prix in an anonymous eleventh place. On his return to the Ferrari pit he was welcomed like a hero by his team and liberally doused in champagne! ■

• **74**_Lauda made an
anonymous start to the French
Grand Prix, which ended in a
spin for the Austrian.
(Roland Kerdilès)

• **75**_Niki or Ricardo, who
is it? The new Brabham-
Cosworth made its debut on
the Ile de Notre Dame circuit
in Montreal on Friday
28th September 1978. Lauda
did a few laps in the car and
then quit the circuit. He left his
team his driving suit and
helmet, which were given to
young Ricardo Zunino who
lapped wearing the champion's
overalls. The identity of the
driver in the photo remains
a mystery.

Chapter 12
1982
Back at the front!

• **77 and 78**_Nike Lauda's comeback in 1982 in the South Africa Grand Prix was notable for two reasons: firstly, his involvement in the Drivers' strike and secondly his encouraging performance on the Kyalami circuit.

auda's fans had resigned themselves to the fact that he was now history and that F1 had seen the back of him. Grand prix racing, in fact, was about to enter a speeded up phase of development. The cars were lapping quicker and quicker thanks to ground effect and the power of the fledgling turbo engine. Things were also hotting up between the English constructors in the FOCA, who were scared that supercharging would send their costs rocketing, and the FISA, which defended the turbo technology. Conflict became inevitable between the two camps; one led by the cunning Bernie Ecclestone and the other by the intransigent, choleric FISA president, Jean-Marie Balestre. 1980 and 1981 saw the battle increase in intensity both on the track and off and a few blows below the belt were struck as tension in F1 reached new heights. In addition, a whole new generation was coming to the fore and the likes of Fittipaldi, Hunt, Scheckter, Andretti and Jones were sidelined by rising stars such as Prost, Villeneuve, Arnoux, Piquet and Pironi. They were the guys who captured public imagination and few observers paid much attention to the discrete presence of Niki Lauda on the Austrian Grand Prix rostrum on 16th August 1981.

For over two years the former world champion had been fully involved in running his air company and had not set foot anywhere near a circuit. His daring initiative had come up against a brick wall, or rather two, in the form of the hike in petrol prices in 1980 and the monopoly of the Austrian national airline company. He was getting a bit bored and started watching grands prix on the television again. So he accepted an invitation from Austrian TV to interview the first three in the race, Jacques Laffite, René Arnoux and Nelson Piquet. His presence did not escape the eagle eye of the new McLaren boss.

The driving ambition of Ronald Dennis was to bring the McLaren International team back to the summit of Formula 1 and he had an original idea of how to do it. With the help of Marlboro he purchased the stagnating Woking outfit from Teddy Mayer at the end of 1980, and presented a daring technical project from the highly inventive mind of John Barnard. The latter, who had already designed the very successful F. Indy Chaparral, came up with the idea of an F1 car with a carbon fibre monocoque. It was a courageous move as

nobody at that time had really mastered this innovative material. Its main advantage was a big reduction in the number of sections needed for the chassis skeleton hence an enormous gain in rigidity without any loss in strength as Andrea de Cesaris, the impetuous McLaren driver, proved by his numerous accidents during the 1981 season. Once this step had been taken Dennis knew that his team would not escape the turbo revolution even though he did not break ranks with his fellow-constructors in the FOCA in their battle with the FISA. He began negotiations with Porsche which resulted in the creation of a V6 turbo engine that was to be built in Stuttgart and financed by the TAG company belonging to the Ojehs, a Saudi family, whose son, Mansour, was a McLaren shareholder. Once the project was under way Ron Dennis started to look round for a top-class test driver to replace the inexperienced de Cesaris alongside John Watson. He knew Niki Lauda well as he had entered him for the Procar Championship, the F1 grand prix curtain raiser in 1979 in a Marlboro-sponsored BMW M1. So naturally, the contacted the ex-champion and asked him to come out of retirement!

• **79**_He showed that he had lost none of his skills in the streets of Long Beach. He chose the right moment to slice past the hot-headed de Cesaris in his Alfa Romeo and went on to score his 19th F1 victory in only his 3rd race after his comeback. It was like he'd never been away!

Designer: John Barnard

Engine

Make/type: Ford Coswoth DFV
No. of cylinders/layout: V8 (rear)
Cubic capacity: 2993 ccs
Bore/stroke: 85.6 x 64.8 mm
Compression ratio: 12:1
Max. power: 480 bhp
Max. revs: 11,100 rpm
Block: Aluminium
Fuel/oil: Unipart
Plugs: Unipart
Injection: Lucas
Distribution: 4 O.H.Cs
No. Of valves per cylinder: 4
Ignition: Lucas/Contactless
Weight: 163 kgs

Transmission

Gearbox/ no. of ratios: McLaren/Hewland (5)
Clutch: Borg & Beck

Chassis

Type: Carbon monocoque
Suspension: rocker arm, coil spring damper, lower wishbone,
front/rocker arm lower wishbone, coil spring dampers, rear.
Dampers: Koni
Wheels diameters: 15" (Front) / 13.38" (Rear)
Rim widths: 11" (Front) / 14.76" (Rear)
Tyres: Michelin
Brakes: Lockheed

Dimensions

Wheelbase: 2682 mm
Tracks: 1816 mm front, Rear not communicated
Dry weight: 580 kgs
Fuel tank capacity: 179.5 litres

Used throughout the season.

Niki was like a ripe fruit, ready for the picking. His enthusiasm for Formula 1 had been rekindled and the prospect of taking up this new challenge after a 2-year absence was one he could not resist. The Italian company Parmalat got wind of the project and promised him its support again. Lauda then met the McLaren boss to discuss the financial aspect of his contract. He remained faithful to his image of being a tough negotiator and the amount he obtained set tongues wagging in the little world of Formula1. He asked for and got two million dollars for his publicity value and accepted a symbolic dollar per grand prix for the 1982 season. The agreement was officially announced in November 1981 and was greeted with general scepticism. For the majority of pundits it was clear that he was only in it for the money especially as his air company was going through a rocky period. This he denied stating that Lauda Air's debts were covered by the

leasing of a couple of Fokkers to an Egyptian company. In addition, he said it was impossible to race for money alone and that he was really motivated. His results would silence the doubting Thomases and there was a clause in the contract that allowed McLaren to get rid of him before the end of the season if his performance was not up to scratch.

After a private test on the Donington circuit on 16th September 1981 in the greatest possible secrecy at the wheel of the McLaren MP4/1 Niki got down to the task of becoming fit enough to drive in a grand prix with the help of his faithful coach Wily Dungl. It should be made clear that although the Austrian was always in impeccable form during his racing career, when he hung up his helmet his love of the good things of life gained the upper hand and there was a few surplus kilos to be lost, and he also needed to recapture his previous level of endurance.

Pierre Dupasquier: "He had his head over the steering wheel".

The manager of the Michelin Competitions Department had a bird's eye view of Niki Lauda's return to racing as the French manufacturer supplied tyres to McLaren. He never had any doubts as to the driver's motivation.

"When he got back into the car for the first time we really didn't know if he still had the same motivation, reflexes and feeling even if Ron Dennis had taken the necessary precautions. His behaviour and involvement left no room for doubt. For example, he sometimes called me at home late in the evening to try and speed up the installation of the turbo engine that Barnard was still reluctant to put in the car. He thought that the sooner the engine was in the McLaren, the sooner we'd collect experience and start winning races. He wanted me to push Ron Dennis and John Barnard to have the engine installed two races earlier than scheduled. He was a real manager and organiser. He had this ability to concentrate all the efforts of the team around him to create a winning machine and he had an incredible ability to read a race. It was almost as if he was looking down from above! Once he made a mistake and collided with Rosberg, I can't remember where, and I said to myself, 'What an idiot! At his age it's not possible!' But it's the only mistake I recall. In addition he had a marvellous ability to nurse a sick car and bring it home. I remember Rio in 1978 when Reutemann scored our first victory (Michelin was supplying tyres to Ferrari). Niki was at the wheel of a Brabham and finished third in a car that was literally falling to bits. Nothing held together, the gearbox was dragging along the ground! A real wreck. After the race he came and congratulated me on the tyres showing that he already trusted our know-how. I returned the compliment saying that he was the only one who could've finished in such a heap!"

• **80**_Pierre Dupasquier is still part of the F1 circus in 2004 and faithful as always to Michelin

In the interseason Lauda racked up a large number of kilometres to get used to handling a grand prix car again as well as coming to grips with the new technical innovations that had appeared while he was away like, for example, the incredibly stiff suspension necessary to cope with the ground effect generated by the new generation F1 cars. Together with his former Brabham team-mate, John Watson, he began to absorb the finer points of the McLaren's composite chassis. As in the past he did not attempt to rush things and bit-by-bit he worked out exactly how it functioned. He had no doubt that he would be ready for 23rd January 1982 the date of the opening round of the world championship on the Kyalami circuit in South Africa.

He did not screw up his comeback either on or off the circuit. He was one of the leaders of the famous drivers' strike* bringing his assurance and experience to the younger members who were worried about the possible fall-out on their careers. Then on race day he finished in fourth place without the slightest problem. For the observers it was a significant achievement after a 2-year absence and showed that his talent was still intact. And what happened in California two months later convinced everybody about the double world champion's potential.

He collided with Reutemann in the Brazilian Grand Prix and then qualified on the front row in Long Beach. Alongside him to everybody's surprise was Andrea de Cesaris in his Alfa Romeo. The Italian made the best start and led the opening laps of the race on the Californian street circuit. However, Lauda used all his race craft to pressure the volatile de Cesaris and on lap 15 out of the 75 Andrea went off line when lapping Boesel's March and Niki sliced past him. In trying to catch Lauda the Alfa Romeo driver hit the wall eight laps later while the no.8 McLaren was going quicker and quicker and when Lauda judged that he was out of harm's way he slowed. In keeping with his principles of nursing his car he lifted off but under his red helmet with the Lauda Air logo the temperature must have risen a notch or two as he exulted. He had put one over on all his rivals as well as on those who had not believed in him. When he took the chequered flag he gave his delighted mechanics a brief wave and parked his car quietly on the side of the track with the feeling of a job well done.

Obviously his win caused a big stir. Lauda had won his bet and his victory made headlines round the world. He was praised to the skies and his victory silenced those who had said that he was only in it for the cash. After all had he not

come back from hell six years previously and won the title the following season when nobody would have bet a penny on him. In fact, it was almost like he had never been away as he triumphed in what were even more difficult circumstances. This guy Lauda was really something else!

The Austrian, however, kept a cool head, as he knew that the McLaren MP4/1's problems were far from being solved. It did not work properly on certain circuits with the Michelin radials. The French tyres had a tendency to flatten at high speeds and thus gave better road holding than the Goodyears provided that the ground clearance was perfectly adjusted. The McLaren's reliability still needed improving as Niki found to his cost in Monaco and Montreal. He managed to finish third at Zolder despite excessive tyre wear (see Watson) but was disqualified, as his car was 1.8 kilos under the minimum weight. In Detroit he hit the wall showing that even he was not immune to silly mistakes. So as the teams tackled the second half of the season he had dropped down the championship ladder on the top step of which was his team-mate John Watson after a couple of victories in Belgium and Detroit. His mind-blowing performance at Long Beach now forgotten the pundits again began to whine. Niki, though, was convinced that his poor results were due to the ups and downs of motor racing rather than any fundamental inadequacies on his part. He drove another brilliant race at Brands Hatch to win the British Grand Prix taking advantage of the mishaps of some of his rivals. He slotted into second behind Nelson Piquet's Brabham, which

was carrying a light fuel load, as 1982 was the year when Niki's former team brought back pit stops. The BT50's Achilles Heel was its 4-cylinder BMW turbo that had an annoying tendency to vomit its intestines all over the track during the race. Thus, Lauda was not terribly worried when it drew away and on lap 9 he was proved right when the Brabham ground to a halt and he went into the lead. That was it. Race over! This victory on a circuit where he had not had much success in the past brought him up to third place in the championship behind Didier Pironi and John Watson.

Things went badly in the French Grand Prix on the Paul Ricard circuit where he could do no better than eighth due to tyre problems and the Cosworth's lack of grunt in relation to the turbos. Then, during practice on the Hockenheim circuit he hit the protective barriers hard when he went off avoiding another car. As he had not let go of his steering wheel in time he suffered from distended ligaments in his wrist. He decided not to race in Germany, as he wanted to be fit for the Austrian Grand Prix, which was the following week. In his home event he finished a disappointing fifth because he was unable to find the right set-up for the long, sweeping curves on the Osterreichring. Then came the Swiss Grand Prix on the Dijon circuit (racing having been banned in Switzerland after the 1955 Le Mans disaster). Niki finished third and with two events to go before the end of the season everything was still possible mathematically speaking but from a practical point of view it looked very difficult for the Austrian. Since Pironi's terrible

• **81**_Lady Luck had never smiled on Lauda at Brands Hatch until 1982 when he won his 2nd grand prix of the season. Although he had now really got the hang of the McLaren MP4/1B he faced stiff opposition from his team-mate, John Watson.

• **82**_He had never been very lucky on his home circuit and 1982 was no exception. The McLaren's handling characteristice were unsuited to the Österreichring's long curves and he failed to shine in front his home crowd.

John Watson: "Niki had a kind of protective membrane in which he cocooned himself."

The Northern Irish driver drove the revolutionary McLaren MP4 with its carbon fibre chassis to its first victory in the 1981 British Grand Prix. In 1982, he again had Lauda as team-mate and he managed to find a hole in the Austrian's seemingly impregnable defence.

"Niki based himself on all he had learnt and absorbed before returning to Formula 1. Whether it was a question of ground effect did not change anything. The bottom line was that he was driving a racing car. He spent hours trying to work things out which he did as he was intelligent. What I learnt from him and used better in 1982 than in 1978 was that kind of safety margin that he had in his driving; if he hadn't tested something he wouldn't use it in a race. He wanted to test first of all and gain experience, which is normal. He defined a kind of zone in which he worked and where he could control his knowledge and information. And there he was very difficult to beat. But if you got him outside this zone and he didn't fully understand he was much more vulnerable. His whole life is like that. When he flies a plane he checks everything thoroughly, leaving nothing to chance and it was the same with the car.

I'll give you a striking example: in the 1982 Belgian Grand Prix – which I won – it was obvious on Sunday morning that our cars were not quick enough. Teddy Mayer, who looked after my McLaren, asked me to use another type of Michelin tyre. 'No way,' I said but they persuaded me to fit them and after a few laps I found that they were pretty good and decided to use them for the race. At the end of the warm up Niki saw how quick I was and asked me what I'd changed. I told him, as I was not one to keep secrets to myself. I added, 'If I were you I'd fit them too.' 'No,' he answered. I said to him, 'you're crazy!' 'I won't do it because I haven't had an opportunity to test them and I can't start in such conditions.' I had tried them and it wasn't that he didn't trust me but it would've meant breaking his concentration and racing in conditions he hadn't envisaged and wasn't prepared for. I won the grand prix in a car that behaved impeccably while he had a problem with his at the front after only a few laps."

accident at Hockenheim the battle for the title raged between Watson and Finn Keke Rosberg but thanks to his victory in the Swiss Grand Prix the latter had opened up a gap over the Northern Irishman. In addition, Wattie had been passed by young Frenchman Alain Prost and was now lying third equal with Lauda one point behind the Renault driver. Las Vegas hosted the final round of the championship and the battle for the title (after Monza) between Watson and Rosberg turned in favour of the Finn. Niki did not expect much from the last two races and retired in both.

Overall in what has been a disastrous season from many points of view with two fatalities (Villeneuve at Zolder and Ricardo Paletti in Canada plus Piroini's career-ending accident on the Hockenheim circuit) as well as the political shenanigans, Lauda's performance was a remarkable one. He came fifth in the F1 Drivers' World Championship scoring two wins, which promised well for 1983 with the arrival of the Porsche engine. He was to make a large contribution to its success. ■

Chapter 13
1983
Waiting for Porsche

• **85**_The McLaren was blown off by the turbocharged cars on the beautiful Spa-Francorchamps circuit which had undergone a facelift.

From Ron Dennis's viewpoint taking on Niki Lauda in 1982 was of capital importance for two reasons; firstly, he was one of the best test drivers around and secondly, his strong personality would be a valuable asset in persuading Porsche to take up the F1 challenge. He was right on both counts.

The company had raced in Formula 1 in 1961 and 62 stopping at the end of that season despite Dan Gurney's victory in the French Grand Prix on the Rouen circuit in an 804.

It had never been very enthusiastic about what was called the pinnacle of motor sport and had made itself famous in endurance racing. Obviously, it was loath to risk its reputation in F1 but when Niki Lauda accompanied Ron Dennis to Stuttgart he used all his technical experience to explain to the people from Porsche just how committed and competent the McLaren team was. The German firm declared its interest making it clear, however, that there was no way it would finance an F1 turbo engine. Should someone wish to put up the cash then serious discussions could begin. At that time TAG owned by Akram Ojeh was the main

Williams sponsor and Dennis managed to persuade Mansour Ojeh, Akram's son, that it would be better to be a part of an F1 company rather than just being a name on a car. He offered him shares in McLaren on the understanding that TAG would finance the Porsche turbo engine. Mansour agreed and once again Lauda's presence proved to be the clincher for the Saudi family. The contract with Porsche was signed on the eve of the Italian Grand Prix in September 1982 resulting in the creation of the company TAG Turbo Engines. This explains why when the 1983 season kicked off the German V6 was far from ready and McLaren had to make do with the old normally aspirated V8 Ford Cosworth, which none of the McLaren staff, Lauda included, was very happy about.

The MP4/1C did not differ from the 1982 B version apart from the obligatory flat bottom introduced to banish ground effect. Alas, the Michelin tyres, problematical in 1982, proved completely incompatible with the car's new aerodynamics which, added to its lack of power, explains why the 1983 season was such a disastrous one in terms of results. The first two

races initially seemed to prove otherwise. In Rio, Niki wearing his familiar red helmet with the Lauda Air logo in white finished third way behind Piquet and Rosberg and in Long Beach he came second behind his team-mate John Watson. The fact that the McLarens scored a resounding double was a surprise in itself but what made it all the more extraordinary was the fact that Watson started from twenty-second

spot on the grid and Lauda from twenty-third! The Michelins, which had proved disastrously slow in practice, were much more resistant in the race. In addition, a number of collisions led to several retirements and thus the way was wide open for the two MP4/1Cs to fight their way to the head of the field. Watson duly won and Lauda went into the championship lead but the fairy tale was about to end.

• **86**_Niki's decision to put pressure on Marlboro to speed up the TAG turbo project did not please Ron Dennis at all. It was a turning point in the relationship between the two men, something that Lauda had perhaps not foreseen.

1983 McLaren MP4C–Ford Cosworth

Same caracteristics as the 1982 MP4/B except:

Engine
Make/Type: Ford Cosworth DFY (short stroke)
Cubic capacity: 2994 ccs
Bore/stroke: 90.00 x 58.8 mm
Compression ratio: 12.2:1
Max. power: 510 bhp
Max. revs: 11,000 rpm
Weight: 145 kgs

Raced from Brasil to Austria.

Chassis
Dampers: Bilsen
Wheel dimaeters: 13" front and rear
Rim widths: 11" (Front) / 16" (Rear)
Brakes: SEP/AP

Dimensions
Wheelbase: 2687 mm
Dry weight: 540 kgs

Niki retired in the next two races after extremely poor practice sessions and then came Monaco. This was the low point of the season for McLaren as neither car qualified! The reason? An erroneous tyre choice on Thursday and rain on Saturday. Niki had had to wait ten years for his first non-qualification! The sooner the V6 turbo arrived the better but this did not seem to dovetail with Ron Dennis's and above all John Barnard's way of seeing things.

John was a perfectionist and since the start of the project he had been working on a completely new car for the German engine. It was taking a lot of time and he did not envisage bringing it out until the start of 1984 to enable him to optimise the tiniest details. Niki did not

agree with this philosophy at all. The way he saw it it was essential to get the engine into the chassis as soon as possible so that the work of ironing out the problems could begin. He wanted to get the car up and running for the final grands prix of a season that was already over to all intents and purposes. A categorical niet was Dennis and Barnard's answer. So throwing his usual caution to the winds Niki turned directly to Marlboro using all his political skills and experience as the cigarette manufacturer was paying for part of the design and build of the engine. The company listened to his arguments and upped the pressure on the McLaren management to have a car ready to race in the shortest possible time. While Niki

• **87**_The new TAG turbo Porsche-powered MP4/1E was the centre of attraction at Zandvoort. It was entrusted to Niki Lauda for what was really an extended test session.

reckoned that he had won the battle his personal approach to Marlboro did not go down at all well with Dennis and Barnard as John Watson recalls: "Niki went to see Marlboro to have them put pressure on John and Ron to install the turbo into the current car. He also put pressure on Butzi (Ferdinand 'Butzi' Porsche, Ferry's eldest son). John Barnard wanted to bring out a special car designed around this engine. Marlboro insisted that he speed things up and he was obliged to bring out an intermediary vehicle. And he was not a happy bunny! John and Ron were so upset by this initiative that when the car ran for the first time on the Weissach test track in Germany I was behind the wheel. It should, of course, have been Niki after all he had done for McLaren." The ambience between Dennis/Barnard and their star driver was frosty

to say the least as the two top dogs at McLaren could not stomach the fact that an employee, no matter how talented, had dictated the way to go. A high degree of pride flirting with inflation is one of the characteristics associated with people who succeed, and no doubt Niki would not have been very happy had the boot been on the other foot. In the present case it was soon easy to see who was right.

When John Watson arrived at the Weissach test track he found a prototype 956 sports car fitted with the V6 turbo, which he tried out to compare it with the McLaren in which the same engine was installed. In fact, Porsche had tested it in secret, a fairly logical step by a manufacturer desirous to gather information as quickly as possible but which sent Ron Dennis into a fit of rage as soon as he heard about it.

• **88**_Lauda and Watson ironed out the faults of the MP4/1E turbo during the final grands prix of the 1983 season. A turbo blew on Niki's car during the European Grand Prix on the Brands Hatch circuit.

Designer: John Barnard

Engine

Make/Type: TAG-Porsche PO1 (TTE PO1)
Number of cylinders/layout: V6 (rear)
Cubic capacity: 1499 ccs
Bore/stroke: not communicated
Compression ratio: 7:1
Turbos: 2, KKK
Max. power: 700 bhp
Max. revs: 11,500 rpm
Block : Aluminium alloy
Fuel/oil: Elf/Unipart
Plugs: Bosch
Injection: Bosch Motronic MS3
Distribution: 4 OHCs
No. of valves per cylinder: 4
Ignition: Bosch Motronic MS3
Weight: 150 kgs (without turbos, intercoolers and exhausts)

Transmission

Gearbox/no. of ratios: McLaren Hewland (5)
Clutch: AP/Borg & Beck

Chassis

Type: Carbon fibre monocoque
Suspension: Rocker arms, coil spring dampers, lower wishbone front/ rocker arms, lower wishbones, coil spring dampers, rear
Dampers: Bilsen
Wheel diameters: 13" front and rear
Rim widths: 11" (Front) / 16" (Rear)
Tyres: Michelin
Brakes: SEP/AP

Dimensions

Wheelbase: 2687 mm
Tracks: 1816 mm (Front) / 1676 mm (Rear)
Dry weight: 540 kgs
Fuel tank capacity: 179.5 litres

Used from the Dutch to the South African Grand Prix.

"The problem was that it was not a Porsche engine, but a TAG-McLaren," explains Watson. *"Porsche had signed a contract to design and build the engine but its rights were held 100% by TAG-McLaren turbo. Porsche had no right to use the power unit for other purposes except with McLaren's permission. But the Germans claimed that it was their engine as they had designed it. Ron made it perfectly clear to them by saying something like: 'I'm very sorry Mr. Porsche it's not a Porsche engine, it's a TAG-McLaren. "We've paid a hell of a lot of money for it and you've abused our trust."* Michel Morelli, a photographer and journalist remembers having attended a session on the Paul Ricard circuit where Walter Röhrl was testing a 956 prototype for Porsche and there was no question of raising the bonnet under the prying eyes of journalists. *"Röhrl found the situation very amusing,"* recalls Morelli. *"We, though, had a pretty good idea of what was in the 956's engine compartment but we didn't have enough proof to put it on paper."*

The intermediary McLaren MP4/1E fitted with the V6 TAG turbo made its official debut in the Dutch Grand Prix on the Zandvoort circuit. It was entrusted to Lauda who had long since abandoned any interest in the Cosworth version which Watson had to make do with. Neither driver saw the finish in the MP4/1E (John got his in Italy) in the last four grands prix of the season but as Lauda had predicted these retirements helped to find the weak spots of car and engine so that the McLaren which lined up for the opening grands prix of the 1984 season was a formidable winning machine. At Zandvoort he went out with brake problems, as those on the MP4/1E were unable to cope with slowing down the car without the help of engine braking – non-existent with a turbo engine. At Monza the electronics went on the blink and at Brands Hatch and Kyalami a short circuit put paid to McLaren's hopes. In South Africa Lauda got up to second place giving a glimpse of the TAG turbo's potential and when the season ended it was with high hopes that the British team began the inter-season test programme with John Banard's latest brainchild the MP4/2. And a big surprise was in store for Niki Lauda!

During the previous two seasons he had got on very well with his team-mate John Watson. The Northern Irishman was a very good driver who had little to envy his Austrian counterpart as well as a loyal team member but he was less adept at setting up the cars, which suited Lauda down to the ground. The Austrian had done most of the sorting out of the McLaren TAG-Porsche and looked forward to the 1984 season with a certain serenity. In short Watson was the ideal team-mate: he was quick and good-humoured but Niki reckoned he could beat him whenever he wanted, a bit like he'd done with Regazzoni at Ferrari. Then in November 1983 Ron Dennis told him that his new team-mate was Alain Prost. You could have knocked the Austrian down with a feather!

John Watson had made a big blunder by delaying his signature on his 1984 contract. He used the pretext that his results were better than those of Lauda in 1982-83 (which was true in terms of championship points and placings) and asked for more money emphasising the big difference in treatment between himself and his team-mate. He had not grasped the fact that the Austrian had deliberately sacrificed his 1983 season in order to ensure that he would be ready to attack 1984 right from the outset. John was now approaching thirty-eight after an excellent career but a very talented youngster had just been unceremoniously booted out of his team and was on the market. The cunning and far-sighted Ron Dennis immediately contacted the Frenchman and offered him a more or less open contract telling Watson that he could not pay him what he wanted. And Niki Lauda saw the young ultra-quick Prost with whom he would have to contend arriving in Woking. He was not very happy about this as it forced him to revise his strategy. ∎

• **89**_Although Niki Lauda retired in the final round of the 1983 championship in South Africa he proved that the McLaren turbo would be a front-runner in 1984. Behind him comes the unfortunate Alain Prost whose title chances bit the dust on the Kyalami circuit where he was trounced by Nelson Piquet, the 1983 champion.

Chapter 14
1984
Niki's third title

• **91**_Niki's face wears a slightly pinched smile as he gives his new team-mate Alain Prost a friendly tap on the shoulder. The Austrian was not too happy about the Frenchman's arrival. However, from a work point of view they soon got on like a house on fire. Prost, though, quickly showed just how quick he was and Niki knew he would have his hands full if he wanted to beat him. In the background are Ron Dennis and Joan Villadelprat, the team's chief mechanic.

When testing kicked off on the Paul Ricard circuit in early 1984 Lauda made sure Prost knew who was boss. He had not done all that work over two years to let a little upstart come in and reap the fruits of his labour. Niki did his testing his own way leaving Prost on the sidelines chewing his nails. A slight uneasiness seemed to be growing between them despite the fact that they had previously expressed mutual esteem in public: *"Niki had a contract as no.1 driver,"* recalls Alain. *"He could have whatever he wanted when he wanted. He was the first to do the testing and could then decide whether to give me the car or not. I've always felt that in life you come from weak or strong positions and that it was up to me to show what I was made of."* In fact, Lauda was unconsciously afraid. He knew just how good Alain was and feared that the Frenchman was there to exploit a stable situation to his own advantage. Niki very soon realised his mistake and discovered that Prost really wanted to build

up a solid team, that he was an unconditional Lauda fan, and also that he assimilated everything at an incredible speed. After that any feeling of suspicion vanished and the two men formed a duo whose complicity had rarely been equalled in the past and would never again be matched in the future.

Respect, though, did not eliminate rivalry. Lauda very quickly spotted his problem with Prost. Throughout his career his greatest strength had always been his capacity to analyse the situations in which he found himself both clearly and intelligently and he then drew conclusions that he applied without hesitation. It did not take him long to understand what was going to happen between himself and Alain. He realised that the Frenchman, who was six years younger, had an insatiable hunger for victory and would be difficult to beat on performance alone so the best way to counter this threat would be meticulous and methodical preparation.

As scheduled the new MP4/2 did not roll out until a few days before the first race of the 1984 season, the Brazilian Grand Prix on the Rio-Jacarepaguä circuit. At the start of the year it looked like being a fairly open championship, as no single team seemed to have a decisive advantage over its rivals even though Renault had lost its star driver. Brabham with world champion Nelson Piquet, Ferrari and the beautiful 126/C4s, the Lotus 95Ts and of course the McLaren MP4/2s all looked well-matched on paper anyway. The Woking team was not the bookies' favourite as it had not had any significant results for quite some time: its cars were too new not to have hidden glitches, the Porsche engine still had to show it was capable of lasting a whole grand prix, and finally, it was rumoured that the relationship between Prost and Lauda was anything but amicable as the Austrian resented the arrival of the Frenchman in the team. However, the results of the first race gave the lie to all these suppositions, and as the year progressed the glaring weaknesses of McLaren's rivals became increasingly evident. Rarely had a team so dominated the F1 World Championship with two such charismatic drivers.

"It was the turbo era," as Prost recalls. *"There were a lot of fuel consumption problems that we got round thanks to Bosch's hard work. The turbo is very tricky. Either it works or it doesn't. It can easily get damaged and its performance falls off. There I was a bit better than Niki. But you know when you're dealing with a guy like Lauda, it goes very quickly. In any case we bonded almost immediately as team-members."*

Victory in the Brazilian Grand Prix, the first round of the championship, went to Prost after Lauda had led for twenty laps and was then let down by electrical gremlins in the engine. Niki was not happy, though, as he wanted to be the first to benefit from all his hard work. Two weeks later he got his revenge in Kyalami but knew that his worries were not over as the Frenchman made a staggering comeback from last to second place proving that the McLarens were the ones to beat and that he was ready to take on the ex-world champion. It was going to be a tough season.

The next two events at Zolder and Imola ended in retirement for Lauda due to mechanical probems. He was starting to get seriously

● **92**_Lauda retired in the opening grand prix in Brazil but he soon put things to rights by scoring a convincing victory in South Africa.

worried as he had finished only once in four races while Prost was romping away with the championship. And what he had foreseen during early testing was coming true: the little Frenchman left him standing in terms of sheer speed. He quickly analysed the situation: either he had to find some extra speed or he could say goodbye to the title in the face of the challenge from his young rival. Prost was showing the full range of his skills a little more each race and was starting to carve out his own niche in the McLaren team. From then on the usually prudent Lauda began to change his driving style, which became more aggressive in the races to compensate for his poorer qualifying positions. Certain drivers noted that he was pushing harder than ever before in a manner that belied his nickname "the computer."

Lauda gave his all on the Dijon-Prenois circuit home to the 1984 French Grand Prix in his efforts to keep up with the leaders Tambay and Prost. His team-mate almost had a huge accident when a wheel collapsed at full speed and when the driver of the black and yellow Renault made a mistake Lauda shot past and sped on to victory. It was his second win of the year and brought him to within six points of Prost who was leading the championship. It all went south for him in the following races, as his meagre reward was six points for a second place in the Canadian event. He suffered engine problems in Detroit and made contact with the scenery in Monaco and Dallas. Honest with himself as always he recognised his errors especially in Monaco where he went off on a very slippery track when third was within his grasp. As the second half of the season approached he evaluated the situation coldly and clearly. He had chalked up two wins as against Prost's three and had made a few mistakes that could prove costly in the final reckoning. However, it was not all gloom and doom as the European circuits that were coming up suited him (and the McLarens) much better than the artificial ones laid out between concrete blocks in American cities. In addition, he was but 10.5 points behind Prost (the Monaco Grand Prix had been stopped prematurely and Prost's haul was only 4.5 points). With a couple of wins and especially if Lady Luck turned against his team-mate-mate anything was possible.

DPPI

Patrick Tambay: "A deadpan Austrian with a touch of British humour".

Patrick Tambay was never Lauda's team-mate but they raced around the same time. The French driver gives a concise summary of this somewhat atypical champion. *"He was and still is his own man, who has never been afraid to assert his own point of view. He always said what he thought. When he retired in 1979 it surprised me that he could give up just like that. It's sure that even if one respected his decision he should've seen his contract through to the end. But it was also proof of his strong character and sense of independence. When he came back I felt that he was efficient, always on the lookout, opportunistic and controlled but not particularly aggressive. He was very good technically speaking and possessed a fine sense of analysis and synthesis: he was very strong on the relationship aspect and his team believed in him. He also had a very caustic sense of humour, which made him different even if he sometimes appeared cold and disdainful. He was a deadpan Austrian with an Anglo-Saxon sense of humour; a rather special mixture in fact."*

And in the British Grand Prix on the Brands Hatch circuit he again saw the chequered flag. He was one happy Austrian on the rostrum especially as neither Prost not Piquet added to their championship tally due to mechanical failure. Two weeks later he notched up another second place in the German Grand Prix which Prost won. Then came his incredible win in the Austrian Grand Prix (see chapter 15) and with it first place in the championship. But was it all sunshine and roses? Well, not exactly as behind the scenes his relationship with Ron Dennis was turning sour.

The McLaren boss had never really stomached the huge sum that he had had to pay Niki to get his name on a contract. At the time Dennis had no choice but to rely on him to bring the development of the McLaren to a successful conclusion. Now things were different: Prost was in the squad and he was much cheaper. Ron explained all this to Lauda and offered him a much lower salary for 1985. The latter refused and began preliminary negotiations with Gerard Larrousse, the Renault team manager, as the French outfit was in deep

trouble and needed someone like Lauda to boost its chances of victory. In addition, the Austrian saw this as a very profitable way to bow of racing with the team that had brought the turbo into F1 in the first place. Lauda continued to meet Larrousse(in secret) to discuss his 1985 contract.

"In particular, we spoke about him joining us during a lunch at the Crillon where he ate some boiled carrots and a yoghurt," recalls Gérard Larrousse. They reached agreement but Lauda refused to sign until such time as he had won his third title as a precautionary measure in relation to McLaren. The agreement in principle between Lauda and Larrousse fell to pieces because of the drastic financial situation of the Renault company and an increasingly large question mark hung over the F1 programme's survival. Thus, there was no use in paying out a huge amount of money to a star who might not be needed in the not too distant future. As the season was drawing to a close Niki had no choice but to accept Ron's offer, which was not as low as the original one thanks to a sweetener from Marlboro.

• 94_His second win of the season came in the French Grand Prix on the Dijon-Prenois circuit just at the right time as it put him back to within striking distance of his young team-mate, the championship leader.

• **95**_After the start of the 1984 British Grand Prix Lauda found himself in 4ᵗʰ place behind Elio de Angelis in his Lotus-Renault, Alain Prost and Nelson Piquet in the lead in his Brabham-BMW. The first two retired with engine problems and the Italian ran into tyre trouble so Lauda went on to score his 3ʳᵈ win and took the lead in the F1 world championship.

In Italy Lauda racked up his fifth success of the season and now led Prost by 10.5 points. Only two races remained, one on the new Nürburgring and the other on the Estoril circuit in Portugal; two tracks with which the majority of the F1 teams were unfamiliar. Prost notched up an easy win on what was still called the 'Ring even though it was a horrible parody of the original. Niki could do no better than fourth after a spin caused by an error of judgement when passing a tail-ender, which shot his tyres to pieces. So only 3.5 points separated the McLaren duo as this enthralling battle entered its final round. Mathematically speaking the Frenchman's chances were intact but Niki had an ace up his sleeve: he knew their cars were the best and that should Prost win all he needed was a second place to score his third F1 world championship title. In practice Prost was in

scintillating form and set the second quickest time while Niki could do no better than eleventh! This put him in a nightmarish position for the race as nothing had gone according to plan what with his engine suddenly losing all its water and his tyres destroyed under heavy braking. However, hope sprang afresh in the warm up as he was quickest overall ahead of Prost. So if he used his legendary patience and took advantage of his opponents' mistakes a second place was on the cards as Prost had shown in South Africa.

The exciting Portuguese Grand Prix was a kind of digest of all Lauda's skills. He made a prudent start avoiding an accident with the rambunctious mid-field scrappers, brought himself up to speed with his first overtaking manoeuvres while whittling down his lap times, showed absolute determination by his somewhat

Designer: John Barnard

Engine

Make/Type: TAG-Porsche P01 (TTE P01)
Number of cylinders/layout: V6 (rear)
Cubic capacity: 1489 ccs
Bore/stroke: not communicated
Compression ratio: 7.5:1
Turbos: 2, KKK
Max. power: 750 bhp
Max. revs: 11,500 rpm
Bloc: Aluminium alloy
Fuel/oil: Shell
Plugs: Bosch
Injection: Bosch Motronic MS3
Distribution: 4 OHCs
No. of valves per cylinder: 4
Ignition: Bosch Motronic MS3
Weight: 145 kgs (without turbos, intercoolers, exhausts)

Transmission

Gearbox/no. of ratios: McLaren Hewland (5)
Clutch: AP/Borg & Beck

Chassis

Type: Carbon monocoque
Suspension: Top link, top rocker arms, coil spring dampers, lower wishbones, front/ top link, rocker arms, coil spring dampers, lower wishbones, rear.
Dampers: Bilstein
Wheel diameters: 13" front and rear
Rim widths: 11.75" (Front) / 16.25" (Rear)
Tyres: Michelin
Brakes: McLaren/SEP

Dimensions

Wheelbase: 2794 mm
Tracks: 1816 mm (Front) / 1676 mm (Rear)
Dry weight: 540 kgs
Fuel tank capacity: 220 litres

Used for the whole season.

• **96**_On the Brands Hatch rostrum Senna (3rd) acknowledges his master while an amused Derek Warwick looks on.

virile pass of young Swede Stefan Johansson
who lost his front wing in the incident after
which he pushed hard to catch Mansell in
second setting several fastest laps in the
process. On lap 52 out of the 70 it was mission
accomplished when the Brit retired. He did not
need to catch his team-mate firmly installed in
the lead and decided to nurse his car to the
finish. After taking the flag he gave the
McLaren team a brief wave, a longer one to the
cheering spectators, stopped and then went up
onto the rostrum.

The normally reserved Austrian's sparkling
eyes were popping out of his head. He had
won his bet, namely, to make his comeback
two years after being completely cut off from
motor racing, shown that he was as quick as
ever, succeeded in bringing a technical project
and car to a triumphant conclusion and won
his third F1 world championship title. Prost was
obviously disappointed while people both
inside and outside the sport were deeply
impressed by the inner reserves of strength
displayed by the Austrian throughout his
racing career.

Marlene Lauda came to Estoril specially
as she had never attended a grand prix since
that fateful August day in 1976, which had left
her with a deep hatred of racing. She climbed
up onto the rostrum and embraced her
husband to rounds of applause from the crowd.
Everybody, teams, spectators etc. knew that
they had witnessed one of the great moments
in Formula 1 history. ∎

• **99**_So ended a passionately exciting season which had seen an all-out battle between two great drivers in the same team.

Chapter 15
"Putting one over on Piquet"

"A memorable race"
Austrian Grand Prix 19th August 1984

Both Lauda and Prost came to the Österreichring knowing that a win there could have a decisive bearing on the outcome of the championship. The Frenchman wanted to make the break and the Austrian needed victory to hang onto his team-mate: he also wanted to come home first in his home grand prix, something that had eluded him so far. His only success there had been in a Porsche 908 in 1970 and in F1 he had always run into some kind of problem be it mechanical or climatical even though he had set three pole positions in 1974-75 and 77. This year he knew he had the best car as the MP4/2 had already won seven out of eleven races and the championship could not escape Ron Dennis's team. Prost was his most serious rival in the title chase and on this layout he could not ignore Nelson Piquet's very powerful Brabham-BMW if the 4-cylinder engine held together over the race distance, a rare occurrence this season. His other rivals posed less of a threat. The Ferraris were hindered by serious chassis problems, the Renaults were too thirsty while the Lotuses were quick but their drivers lacked consistency. Finally, the Williams was heavily penalised by a poor chassis and its Honda engine was incredibly brutal in the way it delivered its power. So for the other teams it was a question of eating the crumbs that fell from the rich man's table, in this case McLaren's. In practice Prost suffered a blown engine and Lauda was hit with accelerator problems while Piquet blasted round the Österreichring to put himself on pole for the sixth time that season. On the grid Niki ended up fourth behind his team-mate and young Italian Elio de Angelis in his Lotus. In 1984, Prost and Lauda always

privileged race set-up over practice performance as witnessed by their results, and on Sunday morning the two McLarens were once again quickest in the warm up.

The first start was aborted due to a problem with the lights and the grand prix began at 15h00 on Sunday 19th August. Prost and Piquet hit the front immediately while Lauda made a more prudent getaway finishing the first lap in sixth place behind Piquet, Prost, Tambay, Warwick and De Angelis. He was employing his usual tactics, namely, using the opening laps to assess the situation before making his move. Once he felt that himself, his car and the circuit were in perfect harmony it was time to up the pace.

On lap 9 he was third behind Nelson and Alain after a daring overtaking move on Tambay on the outside of the Bosch curve (!). On lap 28 fate intervened in the form of De Angelis's Lotus, which vomited its oil all over the track. The marshals waved their flags and Piquet got through after a serious bout of tail wagging by his Brabham but Prost was not so lucky. In fact, the Frenchman had been obliged to drive with one hand for several laps, his left as his right was holding the gear lever in place, and he was caught out by the slippery track and spun off in the Jochen Rindt curve. His engine stalled and he was unable to restart. Only Piquet now stood between Lauda and victory. Soon he was on the Brabham's tail harrying the Brazilian mercilessly to try and push him into making a mistake. Which he did thirty-ninth time round when lapping Alboreto's Ferrari. His tyres were shot and his car slid wide and that was all Lauda needed to slip through into first place. He quickly pulled away and Piquet knew that the

state of his Michelins was such that any hope of a win was now out of the question. Victory on home territory was within Niki's grasp when suddenly on lap 42 he heard a loud bang at the rear of the car in the middle of the Bosch curve.

The McLaren was in neutral as when he changed into fourth the gear literally disintegrated. A wave of disappointment swept over Lauda and he lifted his hand to wave his rivals past. Then playing around with the lever he managed to find third, 'that'll get me to the pits,' he said to himself. He then tried fourth. Nothing. And after that fifth which worked. Immediately his famous 'computer brain' clicked into action. Without fourth there was no chance of victory but by using third to the maximum and fifth and sixth as little as possible he could carry on and bag a few points helping him to close the gap to Prost. What was sure that thanks to the time lost Piquet would be able to catch and pass him. And then to his astonishment his pit informed him that the Brazilian was not making up any time and remained at a respectable distance.

The two men knew each other's race tactics perfectly. When you are well ahead, you lift off to nurse your car. Lauda realised that Nelson was not aware that he was in trouble and the Brazilian thought that he had slowed voluntarily. If Lauda was right then there was no danger of the Brabham driver attacking him especially with his tyres in such a delicate state. With only a few laps to go the gap remained stable and Niki knew that if his gearbox held out victory would be his. And so it was!

When he got out of his car he was delighted: he had finally triumphed on the Österreichring thirteen years after his pathetic F1 debut there. And furthermore he had won in a car that was crippled and put one over on the facetious Piquet. On the way to the rostrum Niki told Nelson what had happened to him and the latter's mouth sagged open as even with his damaged tyres he could have caught and passed the McLaren. But he didn't know and even today Niki still chuckles about it. ■

• **101**_The usual high-speed traffic jam in the Hella-Licht chicane that follows the uphill pits straight on the Österreichring with Prost leading Piquet followed by Lauda and Senna. In fact, the start was aborted due to a short circuit in the starting lights system. On the restart it was Piquet who hit the front from Prost with Lauda back in 6th place.

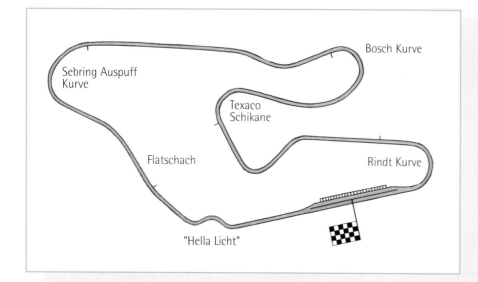

ÖSTERREICHRING, THE CIRCUIT
Permanent circuit
5.942 km / 3.6921 miles

The little town of Zeltweg nestling in the foothills of the Styrian Mountains 5 kms from Knittelfeld and some 50 kms from Graz has a military airfield where national car races were held from 1958 onwards. A group of real enthusiasts looked after the circuit, which soon gained a certain renown, and in 1959 they organised an international F2 race, the *Flugplatzrennen Zeltweg*. Some six well know drivers including Lucien Bianchi, David Piper, Wolfgang Seidel and Carel Godin de Beaufort travelled there and the event was won by Tony Marsh. The following year big names like 2-times F1 champion Jack Brabham, Maurice Trintignant and Stirling Moss came to race on the 3.2 km L-shaped airfield circuit whose perimeters were defined by straw bales. Victory went to Moss. Following the disappearance of F2 in 1961 a race was organised on the Zeltweg circuit for the new 1500 cc F1 cars for which numerous teams turned up with the notable exception of Ferrari. In 1963, the race was included on the international calendar as a non-championship event and the following year it was part of the world championship with victory going to Lorenzo Bandini in his Ferrari. It was the last time that the little aerodrome was used as a circuit as the 1964 race had seen a very high number of breakages caused by the slabs of concrete that were coming apart. The organisers were told that such a circuit could not host a world championship round. This led to the Austrian authorities launching the project of a permanent circuit and they did not have to look very far to find the ideal spot. This was on the flanks of the mountain and a very rapid undulating track was built. Work went quickly and was finished in 1969. The Österreichring was born!

This magnificent circuit initially measured 5,911 kms and welcomed its first F1 grand prix in 1970. It wended its way through the meadows and consisted of long heart-stopping curves that really sorted the men from the boys as setting a good time required all-out attack and millimetric precision in finding the right line in the corners. Out and out speed and good road holding were essential. All the great names like Jackie Ickx, Alain Prost, Jo Siffert, Ronnie Peterson, Alan Jones and Jacques Laffite shone here.

However, the Osterreichring remained a high-risk circuit and in 1975 Mark Donohue lost his life following an accident when his March went straight on in the Hella Licht right-hander. A chicane was installed in 1976 increasing the distance to 5,962 kms. In 1984, the circuit had not evolved and its safety was the object of numerous criticisms, as it no longer complied with the current criteria. It was abandoned by F1 after the 1987 event only to be resurrected in a watered-down version ten years later.

• **102**_Lauda pulls in Piquet whose tyres are beginning to go off. The Austrian took the lead and looked to be heading for an easy win until there was a bang at the back!

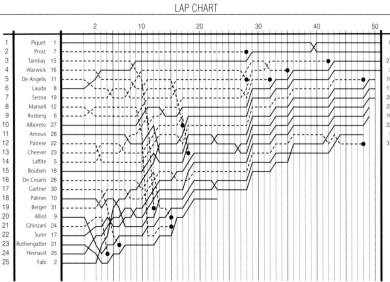

STARTING GRID

1. Piquet 1:26.173	2. Prost 1:26.203
3. De Angelis 1:26.318	4. Lauda 1:26.715
5. Tambay 1:26.748	6. Warwick 1:27.123
7. Fabi 1:27.201	8. Mansell 1:27.558
9. Rosberg 1:28.760	10. Senna 1:29.200
11. Laffite 1:29.228	12. Alboreto 1:29.694
13. Patrese 1:30.736	14. Winkelhock 1:30.853
15. Arnoux 1:31.003	16. Cheever 1:31.045
17. Boutsen 1:31.189	18. De Cesaris 1:31.588
19. Surer 1:31.655	20. Berger 1:31.904
21. Hesnault 1:32.270	22. Gartner 1:33.019
23. Ghinzani 1:33.172	24. Palmer 1:34.128
25. Alliot 1:34.495	26. Rothengatter 1:35.605

• **103**_On the 1984 Austrian Grand Prix rostrum Piquet looks like he's still questioning Lauda about his gearbox problems while the Austrian savours his first (and only) win in front of his home crowd. Third-placed Michele Alboreto seems a bit downcast despite his Ferrari's progress.

RESULTS - 51 race laps for 303.042 kms

1. **Lauda**	**McLaren-TAG**	**51**	**1:21:12.851** 223.883 km/h
2. Piquet	Brabham-BMW	51	1:21:36.376
3. Alboreto	Ferrari	51	1:22:01.849
4. Fabi	Brabham-BMW	51	1:22:09.163
5. Boutsen	Arrows-BMW	50	1 lap
6. Surer	Arrows-BMW	50	1 lap
7. Arnoux	Ferrari	50	1 lap
8. Hesnault	Ligier-Renault	49	2 laps
9. Palmer	RAM-Hart	49	2 laps
10. Patrese	Alfa Romeo	48	Out of fuel
11. Alliot	RAM-Hart	48	3 laps
12. Berger	ATS-BMW	48	3 laps

RETIREMENTS

Tambay	Renault	42	Engine
Senna	Toleman-Hart	35	Oil pressure
Mansell	Lotus-Renault	32	Engine
Prost	McLaren-TAG Porsche	28	Spun and stalled
De Angelis	Lotus-Renault	28	Engine
Rothengatter	Spirit-Hart	23	Turbo
Cheever	Alfa Romeo	18	Engine
Warwick	Renault	17	Engine
De Cesaris	Ligier-Renault	15	Injection
Rosberg	Williams-Honda	15	Road holding
Laffite	Williams-Honda	12	Engine
Gartner	Osella-Alfa Romeo	6	Engine
Ghinzani	Osella-Alfa Romeo	4	Gearbox

FASTEST RACE LAP

Lauda	McLaren-TAG Porsche	1:32.882 230.305 km/h

_LAUDA'S PERFORMANCE IN THE AUSTRIAN GRANDS PRIX

YEAR	CIRCUIT	QUALIFYING	POSITION IN RACE	CAR
1971	Österreichring	21st	Retired (road holding)	March-Ford
1972	Österreichring	21st	10th	March-Ford
1973	Österreichring	Withdrew (injury)	-	BRM
1974	Österreichring	**Pole**	Retired (engine)	Ferrari
1975	Österreichring	**Pole**	6th	Ferrari
1976	Österreichring	Withdrew (injury)	-	Ferrari
1977	Österreichring	**Pole**	2nd	Ferrari
1978	Österreichring	12th	Retired (accident)	Brabham-Alfa Romeo
1979	Österreichring	4th	Retired (oil leak)	Brabham-Alfa Romeo
1982	Österreichring	10th	5th	McLaren-TAG Porsche
1983	Österreichring	14th	6th	McLaren-TAG Porsche
1984	Österreichring	4th	**1st**	McLaren-TAG Porsche
1985	Österreichring	3rd	Retired (engine)	McLaren-TAG Porsche

Chapter **16**
1985
Don't look back!

• 105_Lauda began to ask
himself serious questions
about his F1 future in Monaco
where he had already won
twice.

• 106_ *"This time I've made
up my mind; I'm getting out."*
On the morning of the first
day's practice for the 1985
Austrian Grand Prix Niki Lauda
annouced to the assembled
journalists that he was quitting
F1 at the end of the year. Ron
Dennis knew he could count
on Keke Rosberg for 1986.

Niki Lauda's third F1 title in 1984 transformed him into a super hero. This feat that nobody would have thought possible in 1982 made him a part of motor racing legend alongside dicers like Fangio, Clark, Moss and Stewart to name the most charismatic. For the Austrian it was water off a duck's back as he did not give a damn about statistics. All his concentration was on the coming season as he was well aware that there were a number of variables that would have a direct influence on the outcome of the championship. Would the McLaren-TAG Porsches be as dominant as in 1984? How much progress had their rivals made? And would he be up to the task of retaining his place as no.1? The opening grands prix of the 1985 season gave him a partial answer to these questions.

His rivals had closed the gap. Ferrari and its star driver Michele Alboreto were particularly consistent and quick and Senna's prodigious skills blossomed in the superb Lotus 96 designed by Gérard Ducarouge. The Williams were even faster than the previous year though still hindered by poor reliability and only Brabham seemed to have fallen even further behind. In the opening race of the season in Rio Prost showed that his

motivation was stronger then ever and that the McLaren MP4/2B was capable of racking up victories. For the Austrian, though, it was all beginning to go south.

In early testing it was obvious that the new version of the MP4 had a traction problem at the rear. The big wings with side-mounted winglets had been banned and now the cars were fitted with a simple wing with shorter side plates. All the teams were faced with the same dilemma but it posed particular problems for John Barnard. Not only did the McLaren designer have to cope with this but in addition the cars were now using Goodyear tyres after Michelin's sudden withdrawal at the end of 1984. He found a solution as the year advanced. Niki, though, seemed to be the hardest hit as his young team-mate scored a couple of brilliant wins at Rio and in Monaco (he also won at Imola but was disqualified as the car was under the weight limit). In the Principality the Austrian's problems in coming to grips with the car had not been helped by four retirements due to gearbox problems, which also hit his V6 Porsche at Imola, but he managed to struggle on to the finish. Had he lost his legendary technical feel, which had always enabled him to anticipate and overcome

difficulties? In Monaco he thought about giving up for the first time since his comeback. And it was there in the twisty streets of the Principality that the dangers of driving a single-seater, which put out some 1000 bhp, really hit home. When a driver starts to worry about the dangers of his profession doubt creeps in and his performance suffers accordingly. Those who drive flat out don't ask themselves this kind of question.

After Monaco he ran up a string of five retirements and that was the straw that broke the camel's back. He had had enough and did not seem able to find the same motivation as the previous year. Once he had won his bet it all seemed a trifle superficial to him. Prost was battling with Alboreto for the title lead and he was down in a lowly fourteenth place with three points from his Imola finish. It was time to leave but he did not want to repeat the same mistake as in Montreal in 1979. He would honour his contract to the bitter end and do his best to win a race or two before hanging up his red and white helmet. At the German Grand Prix he informed Ron Dennis of his decision and the latter quickly recruited Keke Rosberg to replace him. Niki was thus free to announce his decision to the press at the following grand prix, which just happened to his home race.

On Friday at 9h00 Lauda told the journalists massed under a tent in the Österreichring paddock that he was quitting. News quickly spread around the paddock and all the drivers agreed that the retirement of the charismatic Austrian would be a big blow to F1 as well as praising his exceptional achievements. Lauda usually did not pay much attention to compliments but even he could not remain unmoved by the homage of his fellow racers starting with his team-mate Alain Prost. Maybe it was relief at having got rid of this burden but he suddenly found his old speed again on the track where he had made his debut in 1971. He was third quickest in practice and passed Prost to take the lead, which he held for eleven laps until a shaft in one of the turbos failed. A very angry Austrian left the circuit before the end of the event. A week later at Zandvoort Lauda was all smiles on the rostrum as he had won his twenty-fifth grand prix fending off the attacks of Prost who was stuck to his gearbox throughout the race. Never during the last 20 laps did the old fox give the young wolf the slightest opportunity to slip past in what was a thrilling duel even if the instructions concerning the turbo pressure somehow slipped the leader's memory (see insert).

• **107**_Niki Lauda fends off Alain Prost on the long Zandvoort pit straight.

Alain Prost:
"Niki wanted one more victory."

The 4-times world champion recalls the 1985 Dutch Grand Prix where he could not pass Niki Lauda and with good reason.
"We were authorised to increase the pressure a little to overtake but otherwise we had to keep to what had been agreed. In 1984 and 85 Niki came to check my figures on a couple of occasions because he was sure that I'd used a little extra boost. He did not respect orders at Zandvoort in 1985. He blocked me throughout the race by using much more turbo pressure than I did. I was a bit upset by the way he did it but there's no need to make a song and dance about the incident. There were never any team orders or the slightest problem and there was none this time either. Quite simply I'd never been world champion and I really wanted that victory. Him too. It was his last and he felt it. On the straight he just walked away from me as he broke the rule about winning whereas I'd never done it. I remembered the incident with Arnoux in the 1982 French Grand Prix when he was still in the lead. I said to myself that I'd always played by the book and it's true I was angry. But it was nothing to do with the fact that he wouldn't let me past as I've read somewhere. When I spoke to him about it as we got out of our cars he said: 'I really wanted to win that race. You won't need me to be champion but if necessary I'll help you.' Eight days earlier he'd told me he was stopping. We always got on very well together as we both improved the engine and chassis; and we also had a great time outside racing."

• **108**_Lauda took the lead in his national grand prix on the Österreichring where he had made his F1 debut fourteen years earlier. His hopes of another win in his home race were thwarted by a blown turbo.

The euphoria of Zandvoort quickly dissipated. At Monza Lauda was never in the ballpark and in Belgium he dislocated his thumb in an accident. This put him out for five weeks and he was obliged to cede his place in the MP4/2B to John Watson. Thus, he saw his team-mate Alain Prost being crowned world champion on TV after the European Grand Prix on the Brands Hatch circuit. There were only two races left, South Africa and Australia. For

some they might have been a formality. But not for Lauda. He wanted to go out on a high with a final win and also to fight off temptation. Bernie Ecclestone had just lost his star driver, Nelson Piquet, to Williams and offered Lauda six million dollars to go back on his decision and drive for Brabham in 1986! Niki, who had always pretended that he did not race for money, began to do some serious head scratching.

Designer: John Barnard

Engine

Make/Type: TAG-Porsche PO1 (TTE PO1)
No. of cylinders/layout: V6 (rear)
Cubic capacity: 1489 ccs
Bore/stroke: not communicated
Compression ratio: 7.5:1
Turbos: 2, KKK
Max. power: 800 bhp
Max. revs: 12,000 rpm
Block: Aluminium alloy
Fuel/oil: Shell
Plugs: Bosch
Injection; Bosch Motronic MP14
Distribution: 4 OHCs
No. of valves per cylinder: 4
Ignition: Bosch Motronic MP14
Weight: 145 kgs (without turbos, intercoolers, exhausts)

Transmission

Gearbox/no. of ratios: McLaren (5)
Clutch: AP

Chassis

Type: Carbon monocoque
Suspension: Top link, push rods, lower wishbones, coil spring dampers, front/
push rods, lower wishbones, coil spring dampers, rear
Dampers: Bilstein
Wheel diameters: 13" front and rear
Rim widths: 11.75" (Front) / 16.25" (Rear)
Tyres: Goodyear
Brakes: McLaren/SEP

Dimensions

Wheelbase: 2794 mm
Tracks: 1816 mm (Front) / 1676 mm (Rear)
Dry weight: 540 kgs
Fuel tank capacity: 220 litres

Used throughout the season.

In the meantime he made his comeback on the Kyalami circuit and had to deal with the turbo problems caused by the altitude plus Ron Dennis's very uncooperative behaviour as the McLaren boss refused him the use of the spare car for practice and the race. He soon realised that his driver was not prepared to be treated like dirt and gave in. Niki qualified mid-field but as usual he had fettled in his car for the race. He then climbed up the field and was soon in third place behind Mansell and Prost. After tyre changes he was second. At half-distance when Nigel shot into his pit for fresh rubber Niki was about to take the lead when a turbo suddenly lost pressure. It was another enormous disappointment for the Austrian; now he had only one chance of scoring that final victory. To put it simply, he didn't. In the streets of Adelaide he drove another excellent tactical race that was worthy of his legend climbing from sixteenth to first place. His rivals suffered from tyre and brake problems and the cunning world champion quietly worked his way to the front. Alas, he suddenly realised that seeing the flag would be a miracle: he still had another thirty laps to cover and his brakes were

becoming increasingly erratic. On lap 57 the pedal went straight to the floor at around 300 km/h at the end of the long Decquetteville Avenue straight. He stabbed the pedal even harder and his rear wheels locked. The McLaren slewed sideways and slammed into the concrete wall. Luckily, Niki had the reflex to lift his hands off the steering wheel and only his pride was hurt. He got out of his wrecked car, waved to the crowd and went back to the paddock. He said goodbye to everybody and took off in a helicopter that brought him to the airport. This new, abrupt departure was for a precise reason.

He was not completely convinced that retiring was a good idea. Ecclestone's offer, his excellent performances at the end of the season, the emotion he felt when he realised he was about to leave a milieu, which he liked, were all very alluring enticements to continue. But he had decided to stop and had to keep to his decision otherwise his credibility would be shot to hell. Thus, to avoid the sense of nostalgia that invaded the paddock on that sunny Sunday afternoon he knew that the only thing to do was to get away as quickly as possible and leave without looking back. ■

• **109**_After sixteen years' racing including twelve in F1 Niki Lauda said *"Auf Wiedersehen"* to the public on 16ᵗʰ November 1985 in the Australian Grand Prix held in the streets of Adelaide for the first time. A chapter in F1 history was closed.

Chapter 17
1986-2003
From Horses
to Jaguars

● **111**_Niki Lauda returned to racing in the early 90s as a consultant with Ferrari. Here he listens to Jean Todt while Berger's eyes wander elsewhere. Pretty woman perhaps?!

And so Niki Lauda bowed out for the second time in his career leaving behind him a glorious legacy even if his final season was not in keeping with his expectations despite a brilliant victory. His willpower, his determination and his incredible ability to move mountains will never be forgotten. The Lauda method can be summed up in the words: observe, study, apply the right tactics, ignore all irrelevancies and win! While some found his approach robot-like, he nearly always confounded his detractors. No team that wanted results could afford to disregard such a talent.

In 1985, the Austrian's last season with McLaren Prost fought a tough battle with Michele Alboreto's Ferrari, at least during the first two-thirds of the season. After that the red car was hit by a succession of mechanical failures, which dashed the Scuderia's title hopes. Ferrari

was beginning its downhill slide and that continued until Prost's arrival in 1990. This was supposed to be the electric shock that would put the Maranello cars back on the road to victory. And he almost succeeded as in 1990 the Frenchman came within a hair's breadth of winning the title. 1991, on the other hand was a catastrophe as the Italian team fell back into its old self-destructive ways firing the wrong people left right and centre. The situation became intolerable for Gianni Agnelli and he acted immediately as in 1973 recalling the man who had done the job in that era, Luca di Montezemolo. Faced with such a disaster di Montezemolo became the director of Automobiles Ferrari and was given a free hand to do what he thought necessary. Before acting one way or another he needed to sort out the different viewpoints and receive advice. Niki

Lauda was still to be seen on the grand prix trail in his famous Parmalat cap and Luca felt that he was ready to play an active role in F1 again.

The Austrian accepted his friend's offer and became Ferrari's special advisor but on the grand prix scene only. He still had Lauda Air to run and that was a full time job in itself so he had only a certain amount of time to devote to the Scuderia. At the start of the 1992 season the former champion was back in the pits. It was a crucial year for the Italian team especially as a revolutionary new car had just come off the drawing board, the F92A to be driven by a couple of hot-blooded Latins, Jean Alesi and Ivan Capelli. Early hopes quickly turned to bitter disillusion and the arrival of John Barnard at the end of the season to put the technical team back on the straight and narrow, did nothing to change the situation. 1993 was almost as bad as 1992 except that a small glimmer of hope appeared on the horizon in the stocky shape of Jean Todt who had masterminded Peugeot's world titles in rallies and endurance. The Auvergnat's orders were simple: put the Prancing Horse back in the winner's circle whatever the cost! Immediately a question mark appeared over Niki Lauda's role. He had not really convinced Ferrari watchers that his presence was of prime importance. Todt's reorganisation plans included a staff clean-out and clearly defined responsibilities. It was time for Lauda to get back to his planes. He stayed on a little longer in the paddock helping the drivers to resuscitate the Grand Prix Drivers Association in 1994 after the Imola accidents, and in 1995 he put all his efforts into persuading double world champion Michael Schumacher to join Ferrari. Which he did for the 1996 season but by then Niki had gone.

It seemed that he could not make a clean break with the F1 milieu and so he managed to find a job as commentator for the German TV channel RTL while remaining director of Lauda Air. However, the situation of his company soon took a turn for the worse as at the end of the 90s the national airline company, Austrian Airlines, got what it wanted after a 20-year struggle, control of Lauda Air. It became obvious that the post of manager offered to the ex-president was a poisoned chalice on a more or less short-term basis. Then at the start of 2001 Niki Lauda found himself in total disagreement with his board of directors and resigned (according to some sources he was fired). So once again his future was in the hands of fate. It did not take long before an offer came up. And what an offer! It was made to him by Wolfgang Reitzle, the Jaguar managing director and Ford vice-president.

• **112**_Following the tragic Imola weekend in 1994 the drivers attempted to close ranks to force the FIA to take safety measures. Lauda served as guide.

The American giant had bought the Stewart team at the end of 1999 from father and son, Jackie and Paul in an attempt to show that American style management was a hell of a lot better than a former F1 champion's. Well, hellish is the right adjective to describe it, as after all the ballyhoo surrounding the launching of the cat into the F1 arena, the 2000 season was a fiasco when comparing the performances of the green cars with the white ones the previous year. In an attempt to strengthen the management side Ford brought in American team owner, Bobby Rahal, to back up Neil Ressner. Rahal was supposed to begin at the start of 2001 and then came an upset. Ressner was obliged to give up his job for family reasons leaving the post vacant. Wolfgang Reitzle had a ready-made solution. He had just the man for the job; someone who had enormous F1 experience and was just waiting for the chance to make a comeback.

So Lauda packed his bags and set off for England and Milton Keynes, the headquarters of Jaguar Racing. He was appointed director of

Premier Performance and under his orders were Jaguar, Cosworth Engineering and Pi Research looked after by Bobby Rahal, Trevor Crisp and Tony Purnell respectively. Unfortunately, the arrival of the much-touted 'saviour' was not translated into success straight away and the Jaguars driven by Eddie Irvine and Pedro de La Rosa did little better than the previous year. Niki then decided it was time to shake the coconut tree and fired Rahal from his job as team manager in August 2001 taking on this responsibility for himself with Ford's backing. He asked his technical team led by Steve Nichols (his former race engineer in the glorious McLaren era) to speed up the design of the new R3, which was to revolutionise the venerable British team.

When the car was presented to the press in January 2002 he announced in his inimitable German accent that it was the fruit of "extraordinary team work." Was it to convince himself that this was true or just a reason to taste the pleasure of driving a Formula 1 car again? Whatever the case he drove a few laps of

• **113**_Among his tasks at Ferrari was to use all his persuasive talents to convince world champion Michael Schumacher to leave Benetton and join the Scuderia.
(Alois Rottensteiner)

• **114**_Lauda left Ferrari and in 2001 he accepted Ford's offer to manage the Jaguar team which was going down the tubes. It was a tricky job and he did not have time to finish it.

the Valencia circuit in the new R3 in February. It was the first time since 1985 that nostalgia buffs could admire the famous red helmet (excepting an outing a few years before in the McLaren two-seater when he gave his sons, Lukas and Matthias, their F1 baptism). Matthias then decided to take up racing in 2002 in the Formula Nissan category. This little self-indulgence punctuated by a couple of spins that made Eddie Irvine double up with laughter proved to the Jaguar boss that his glorious past as a driver had long since vanished into the

● **115**_At the start of 2002 Niki got back behind the wheel of an F1 car, the R3 Jaguar on the Valancia circuit in Spain. Officially it was to test the beast but it would have been more apt to use the expression 'to have a bit of fun!'

mists of time, and that a few laps in a car that he was unable to master, were largely insufficient to judge its potential. Only the 2002 season would prove him right or wrong.

It needed only a few grands prix to prove him wrong: the "extraordinary team work" had produced a car that was a complete dud especially in the area of aerodynamics. Once again he used the strong-arm method and fired Steve Nichols, the technical director, and took on Günther Steiner instead. The latter with one eye on 2003 tried to give some semblance of competitiveness to a dreadful car, and against all expectations his remedy began to work towards the end of the season when the Jaguar R3s performed in a way that was more in

keeping with Ford's expectations as proved by Eddie Irvine's excellent third place on the Monza circuit. The R4 programme was already well under way and the car looked like being much more competitive than its predecessors thanks to the measures taken by Lauda when yet another explosion rocked the English team. On 26th November 2002 the Austrian was shown the door in no uncertain fashion by Richard Parry-Jones, the new Ford vice president, who nominated Tony Purnell in his place. Parry-Jones argued that it was necessary to have a boss who was better versed in current technology while Lauda muttered about an Anglo-Saxon plot. Aged fifty-three the adventurer's future was once again in the hands of destiny.

Lauda's setback as team manager obviously damages his reputation as the great champion he once was but poses the question: does an ex-F1 driver of the highest class make a good team manager? Examining the recent past the answer must be no. Only Jack Brabham and Bruce McLaren have managed to succeed in both fields and for the latter his premature death may have had an influence. The real champions are very stubborn individuals, which is vitally necessary behind a steering wheel but may be a defect when it comes to teamwork. Do they listen enough, do they trust enough, to they delegate when necessary? There are no clear-cut answers to these questions.

Niki Lauda always advocated a radical approach and was someone who said what he thought. He forged a way of working which suited him down to the ground and enabled him to solve the intricate technical problems involved in setting up a car. He was no stranger to open conflict and often acted in a very abrupt manner. His totally fearless attitude allowed him to knock on Enzo Ferrari's door without a prior appointment and talk man to man with a living legend who put the fear of god into his collaborators. He also faced down the conceited Ron Dennis to get what he wanted. John Watson said this about Lauda: "With Niki it doesn't matter what's been written in the contract, he'll get what he wants in the end." All this is applicable to the exceptional driver that he was but was not appropriate for the team manager he aspired to be.

The conclusion to the story is best supplied by Niki himself: never give up because of a setback. After being chucked out of Jaguar at the end of 2002 he came up with a new challenge in November 2003, an airline named Flyniki! Whether it is a question of cars or planes his drive remains intact. ■

• **116**_Would his sons Lukas and Matthias follow in their father's footsteps? The answer is yes as Matthias (on the right) had already begun racing.
(Alois Rottensteiner)

STATISTICS

Victories and titles:

1968 Hill climbs (Mini Cooper 1300),
3 category victories
Hill climbs (Porsche 911),
3 category victories
Circuits, 1 victory (all categories)
1969 Formula V, 2 victories
1970 Sports Cars (Porsche 908), 2 victories
1971 2-litre sports cars (Chevron-Hart), 1 victory
1972 Formula 2 (March 722), 1 victory

1973 Touring cars (BMW-Alpina), 3 victories
Touring Cars (Group 1, BMW 2002), 1 victory
Touring cars (Ford Capri RS), 1 victory
1975 **Formula 1 World Champion**
1977 **Formula 1 World Champion**
1984 **Formula 1 World Champion**

171 Grands Prix
3 F1 World Championship titles
25 victories, 24 pole positions, 25 fastest race laps.

1971__ March 711-Ford in Austria

Tyres Firestone

GRAND PRIX		CIRCUIT	QUALIFYING	RESULT	RACE LAP
1. Austria	17th August	Österreichring	21st (1:43.68)	Rtd (road-holding)	20th (1:45.86)

Position in World Championship: not classified

1972__ March 721-Ford in Argentina and South Africa
March 721X-Ford from Spain to Belgium
March 721G-Ford from France to United States

Tyres Goodyear

GRAND PRIX		CIRCUIT	QUALIFYING	RESULT	RACE LAP
1. Argentina	23 January	Buenos Aires	22nd (1:15.92)	11st at 2 laps	-
2. South Africa	4 March	Kyalami	21st (1:18.90)	7th at 1 lap	-
3. Spain	1st May	Jarama	25th (1:13.76)	Rtd (blocked accelerator)	25th (1:29.84)
4. Monaco	14 May	Monaco	22nd 1:25.60)	16th at 6 laps	-
5. Belgium	4 June	Nivelles-Baulers	25th (1:16.50)	12th at 3 laps	-
6. France	2 July	Charade	21st (3:03.10)	Rtd (half-shaft)	24th (3:23.00)
7. Great Britain	15 July	Brands Hatch	19th (1:25.10)	9th at 3 laps	18th (1:26.50)
8. Germany	30 July	Nürburgring	23rd (7:32.20)	Rtd (oil tank)	-
9. Austria	13 August	Österreichring	21st (1:39.04)	10th at 1 lap	-
10. Italy	10 September	Monza	20th (1:38.52)	13th at 5 laps	-
11. Canada	24 September	Mosport	19th (1:16.80)	Disqualified (outside help)	-
12. United States	8 October	Watkins Glen	25th (1:45.29)	19th at 10 laps	-

Position in World Championship: not classified

1973__ BRM P160 in Argentina and Brazil
BRM P160D in South Africa
BRM P160E from Spain to United States

Tyres Firestone

GRAND PRIX		CIRCUIT	QUALIFYING	RESULT	RACE LAP
1. Argentina	28 January	Buenos Aires	13th (1:12.39)	Rtd (oil pressure)	11st (1:13.07)
2. Brazil	11 February	Interlagos	13rd (2:35.10)	8th at 2 laps	-
3. South Africa	3 March	Kyalami	10th (1:17.14)	Rtd (engine)	9th (1:18.41)
4. Spain	29 April	Barcelone-Montjuich	13th (1:24.40)	Rtd (Blocked wheel nut)	14th (1:26.40)
5. Belgium	14 May	Zolder	14th (1:24.51)	5th at 1 lap	5th (1:25.69)
6. Monaco	3 June	Monaco	6th (1:28.50)	Rtd (gearbox)	10th (1:30.40)
7. Sweden	17 June	Anderstorp	15th (1:26.211)	13th at 5 laps	15th (1:28.708)
8. France	1st July	Paul Ricard	17th (1:51.78)	9th at 1:45.76	10th (1:53.18)
9. Great Britain	14 July	Silverstone	9th (1:17.40)	13th at 5 laps	9th (1:19.60)
10. Holland	29 July	Zandvoort	11th (1:21.43)	Rtd (fuel pump)	-
11. Germany	5 August	Nürburgring	5th (7:9.90)	Rtd (accident)	-
12. Austria	19 August	Österreichring	Withdrew (injured)	-	-
13. Italy	9 September	Monza	15th (1:37.26)	Rtd (accident, wheel)	-
14. Canada	23 September	Mosport	8th (1:15.400)	Rtd (final drive)	-
15. United States	7 October	Watkins Glen	21st (1:43.543)	Rtd (oil pressure)	-

Position in World Championship: 17th / 2 points
Average points per race for season: 0.13

1974_ Ferrari 312 B3/B4

Tyres Goodyear

GRAND PRIX		CIRCUIT	QUALIFYING	RESULT	RACE LAP
1. Argentina	13 January	Buenos Aires	8th (1:51.81)	2nd at 9.27	2nd (1:52.44)
2. Brazil	27 January	Interlagos	3rd (2:33.77)	Rtd (engine)	-
3. South Africa	30 March	Kyalami	Pole (1:16.58)	Rtd (ignition)	MTC (1:18.24)
4. Spain	28 April	Jarama	Pole (1:18.44)	1st 2:00:29.56	MTC (1:20.83)
5. Belgium	12 May	Nivelles-Baulers	3rd (1:11.04)	2nd at 0.35	3rd (1:11.56)
6. Monaco	26 May	Monaco	Pole (1:26.30)	Rtd (alternator)	3rd (1:28.80)
7. Sweden	9 June	Anderstorp	3rd (1:25.161)	Rtd (gearbox)	9th (1:28.437)
8. Holland	23 June	Zandvoort	Pole (1:18.31)	1st 1:43:0.35	5th (1:21.69)
9. France	7 July	Dijon-Prenois	Pole (58.79)	2nd at 20.36	3rd (1:00.50)
10. Great Britain	20 July	Brands Hatch	Pole* (1:19.70)	5th at 1 lap	MTC (1:21.10)
11. Germany	4 August	Nürburgring	Pole (7:00.80)	Rtd (accident)	-
12. Austria	18 August	Österreichring	Pole (1:35.40)	Rtd (engine)	11st (1:28.08)
13. Italy	8 September	Monza	Pole (1:33.16)	Rtd (engine)	4th (1:34.60)
14. Canada	22 September	Mosport	2nd (1:13.230)	Rtd (accident/susp.)	MTC (1:13.659)
15. United States	6 October	Watkins Glen	5th (1:39.327)	Rtd (road-holding)	-

Position in World Championship: 4th / 38 points
2 victories, 9 pole positions, 4 fastest race laps
Average points per race for season: 2.53

(*) Ronnie Peterson (Lotus) set the same time but after Lauda.

1975_ Ferrari 312 B3/B4 in Argentina and Brazil
Ferrari 312T from South Africa to United States

Tyres Goodyear

GRAND PRIX		CIRCUIT	QUALIFYING	RESULT	RACE LAP
1. Argentina	12 January	Buenos Aires	4th (1:49.96)	6th at 1:19.65	8th (1:52.26)
2. Brazil	26 January	Interlagos	4th (2:31.12)	5th at 1:01.88	3rd (2:35.22)
3. South Africa	1st March	Kyalami	4th (1:16.83)	5th at 28.64	7th (1:18.95)
4. Spain	27 April	Barcelone-Montjuich	Pole (1:23.40)	Rtd (Acc. with Andretti)	-
5. Monaco	11 May	Monaco	Pole (1:26.40)	1st 2:01:21.3	5th (1:29.41)
6. Belgium	25 May	Zolder	Pole (1:25.43)	1st 1:43:53.98	2nd (1:27.33)
7. Sweden	8 June	Anderstorp	6th (1:25.457)	1st 1:59:18.31	MTC (1:28.267)
8. Holland	22 June	Zandvoort	Pole (1:20.29)	2nd at 2.0	MTC (1:21.540)
9. France	6 July	Paul Ricard	Pole (1:47.82)	1st 1:40:18.84	2nd (1:50.62)
10. Great-Britain	19 July	Silverstone	3rd (1:19.54)	8th at 2 laps	4th (1:21.50)
11. Germany	3 August	Nürburgring	Pole (6:58.60)	3rd at 2:23.30	3rd (7:80.00)
12. Austria	17 August	Österreichring	Pole (1:34.85)	6th at 1:27.28	-
13. Italy	7 September	Monza	Pole (1:32.24)	3rd at 23.20	3rd (1:33.80)
14. United States	5 October	Watkins Glen	Pole (1:42.003)	1st 1:42:58.175	2nd (1:43.386)

Position in World Championship:
World Champion / 64.5 Points
5 victories, 9 pole positions, 2 fastest race laps
Average points per race for season: 4.6

1976_ Ferrari 312T from Brazil to West United States
Ferrari 312T2 from Spain to Japan

Tyres Goodyear

GRAND PRIX		CIRCUIT	QUALIFYING	RESULT	RACE LAP
1. Brazil	25 January	Interlagos	2nd (2:32.52)	1st 1:45:16.78	3rd (2:35.84)
2. South Africa	6 March	Kyalami	2nd (1:16.20)	1st 1:42:18.40	MTC (1:18.00)
3. United States West	28 March	Long Beach	4th (1:16.20)	2nd at 42.414	2nd (1:23.625)
4. Spain	2 May	Jarama	2nd (1:18.84)	2nd at 30.97	4th (1:21.26)
5. Belgium	16 May	Zolder	Pole (1:26.55)	1st 1:42:53.23	MTC (1:25.98)
6. Monaco	30 May	Monaco	Pole (1:29.65)	1st 1:59:51.47	2nd (1:30.36)
7. Sweden	13 June	Anderstorp	5th (1:26.441)	3rd at 33.866	-
8. France	4 July	Paul Ricard	2nd (1:48.17)	Rtd (engine/c-shaft)	MTC (1:51.00)
9. Great-Britain	18 July	Brands Hatch	Pole (1:19.35)	1st 1:44:19.66	MTC (1:19.91)
10. Germany	1st August	Nürburgring	2nd (7:07.40)	Rtd (accident)	-
11. Austria	15 August	Österreichring	Withdrew (injured)	-	-
12. Holland	29 August	Zandvoort	Withdrew (injured)	-	-
13. Italy	12 September	Monza	5th (1:42.09)	4th at 19.40	4th (1:42.10)
14. Canada	3 October	Mosport	6th (1:13.060)	8th at 1:12.957	8th (1:14.648)
15. United States	10 October	Watkins Glen	5th (1:44.257)	3rd at 1:02.324	6th (1:43.776)
16. Japan	24 October	Mont Fuji	3rd (1:13.08)	Withdrew	-

Position in World Championship: 2nd / 68 points
5 victories, 2 pole positions, 3 fastest race laps
Average per race: 4.6 points

1977_ Ferrari 312T2 — Tyres Goodyear

GRAND PRIX		CIRCUIT	QUALIFYING	RESULT	RACE LAP
1. Argentina	9 January	Buenos Aires	4th (1:49.73)	Rtd (oil pressure)	8th (1:52.02)
2. Brazil	23 January	Interlagos	15th (2:32.37)	3rd at 1:47.51	14th (2:37.40)
3. South Africa	5 March	Kyalami	3rd (1:16.29)	**1st 1:42:21.60**	2nd (1:17.68)
4. United States West	3 April	Long Beach	**Pole (1:21.650)**	2nd at 0.773	**MTC (1:22.753)**
5. Spain	8 May	Jarama	3rd (1:19.48)	Forfait (painful ribs)	-
6. Monaco	22 May	Monaco	6th (1:30.76)	2nd at 0.89	2nd (1:31.58)
7. Belgium	5 June	Zolder	13rd (1:27.11)	2nd at 14.19	7th (1:28.57)
8. Sweden	19 June	Anderstorp	15th (1:26.826)	Rtd (road-holding)	14th (1:28.935)
9. France	3 July	Dijon-Prenois	11st (1:13.52)	5th at 1:14.45	5th (1:14.87)
10. Great Britain	16 July	Silverstone	3rd (1:18.84)	2nd at 18.31	6th (1:20.26)
11. Germany	31 July	Hockenheim	3rd (1:53.53)	**1st 1:31:48.62**	**MTC (1:55.99)**
12. Austria	14 August	Österreichring	**Pole (1:39.32)**	2nd at 20.13	**MTC (1:41.81)**
13. Holland	28 August	Zandvoort	4th (1:19.54)	**1st 1:41:45.93**	**MTC (1:19.99)**
14. Italy	11 September	Monza	5th (1:38.54)	2nd at 16.96	2nd (1:39.60)
15. United States East	2 October	Watkins Glen	9th (1:42.089)	4th at 1:40.615	10th (1:58.924)
16. Canada	9 October	Mosport	Withdrew (sick)	-	-
17. Japan	23 October	Mont Fuji	Withdrew	-	-

Position in World Championship:
World Champion / 72 points,
3 victories, 2 pole positions, 4 fastest race laps
Average per race: 4.5 points

1978_ Brabham BT45C-Alfa Romeo in Argentina and Brazil
Brabham BT46-Alfa Romeo from South Africa to Canada except
Brabham BT46B-Alfa Romeo in Sweden — Tyres Goodyear

GRAND PRIX		CIRCUIT	QUALIFYING	RESULT	RACE LAP
1. Argentina	15 January	Buenos Aires	5th (1:48.70)	2nd at 13.21	3rd (1:50.94)
2. Brazil	29 January	Rio-Jacarepaguà	10th (1:42.08)	3rd at 57.02	3rd (1:43.57)
3. South Africa	4 March	Kyalami	**Pole (1:14.65)**	Rtd (engine)	6th (1:17.43)
4. United States West	2 April	Long Beach	3rd (1:20.937)	Rtd (ignition)	7th (1:22.727)
5. Monaco	7 May	Monaco	3rd (1:28.84)	2nd at 22.45	**MTC (1:28.65)**
6. Belgium	21 June	Zolder	3rd (1:21.70)	Rtd (acc. with Scheckter)	-
7. Spain	4 June	Jarama	6th (1:17.94)	Rtd (engine)	6th (1:20.85)
8. Sweden	17 June	Anderstorp	3rd (1:22.783)	**1st 1:41:00.606**	**MTC (1:24.836)**
9. France	2 July	Paul Ricard	3rd (1:44.71)	Rtd (engine)	8th (1:49.78)
10. Great Britain	16 July	Brands Hatch	4th (1:17.48)	2nd at 1.41	**MTC (1:18.60)**
11. Germany	30 July	Hockenheim	3rd (1:52.29)	Rtd (engine)	12nd (1:57.12)
12. Austria	13 August	Österreichring	12th (1:39.49)	Rtd (accident)	-
13. Holland	27 August	Zandvoort	3rd (1:17.33)	3rd at 12.21	**MTC (1:19.57)**
14. Italy	10 September	Monza	4th (1:38.215)	**1st 1:07:04.54**	4th (1:39.06)
15. United States East	1er October	Watkins Glen	5th (1:39.892)	Rtd (engine)	13rd (1:42.460)
16. Canada	8 October	Montréal-Notre Dame	7th (1:39.020)	Rtd (brakes)	19th (1:42.483)

Position in World Championship: 4th / 44 points
2 victories, 1 pole position, 4 fastest race laps
Average per race: 2.75 points

1979_ Brabham BT48-Alfa Romeo from South Africa to Italy — Tyres Goodyear

GRAND PRIX		CIRCUIT	QUALIFYING	RESULT	RACE LAP
1. Argentina	21 January	Buenos Aires	22nd (1:50.29)	Rtd (fuel pressure)	17th (1:52.65)
2. Brazil	4 February	Interlagos	12nd (2:27.57)	Rtd (gearbox)	-
3. South Africa	3 March	Kyalami	4th (1:12.12)	6th at 1 lap	9th (1:15.95)
4. United States West	8 April	Long Beach	11st (1:20.041)	Rtd (acc. with Tambay)	-
5. Spain	29 April	Jarama	6th (1:15.45)	Rtd (oil leak)	5th (1:18.76)
6. Belgium	13 May	Zolder	13rd (1:22.87)	Rtd (moteur)	13rd (1:24.83)
7. Monaco	27 May	Monaco	4th (1:27.21)	Rtd (acc. with Pironi)	13rd (1:30.26)
8. France	1st July	Dijon-Prenois	6th (1:08.20)	Rtd (spin)	15th (1:12.58)
9. Great Britain	14 July	Silverstone	6th (1:13.44)	Rtd (freins)	18th (1:17.62)
10. Germany	29 July	Hockenheim	7th (1:50.37)	Rtd (brakes)	8th (1:53.12)
11. Austria	12 August	Österreichring	4th (1:35.51)	Rtd (oil leak)	11st (1:38.68)
12. Holland	26 August	Zandvoort	9th (1:17.495)	Rtd (painful hand)	19th (1:23.293)
13. Italy	9 September	Monza	7th (1:35.443)	4th at 54.40	5th (1:37.14)
14. Canada	30 September	Montréal-Notre Dame	withdrew (retired)	-	-
15. United States East	7 October	Watkins Glen	withdrew (retired)	-	-

Position in World Championship: 14th / 4 points
Average per race: 0.226 points

1982_ McLaren MP4B-Ford Cosworth all year

Tyres Michelin

GRAND PRIX		CIRCUIT	QUALIFYING	RESULT	RACE LAP
1. South Africa	23 January	Kyalami	13th (1:10.681)	4th at 32.113	7th (1:10.577)
2. Brazil	21 March	Rio-Jacarepaguà	5th (1:30.152)	Rtd (acc. with Reutemann)	5th (1:37.364)
3. United States West	4 April	Long Beach	2nd (1:27.436)	**1st 1:58:25.318**	MTC (1:30.831)
4. San Marino	25 April	Imola	Team withdrew		
5. Belgium	9 May	Zolder	4th (1:16.049)	Disqualified *	6th (1:20.885)
6. Monaco	23 May	Monaco	12th (1:25.838)	Rtd (engine)	7th (1:27.415)
7. United States East	6 June	Detroit	10th (1:51.026)	Rtd (accident)	3rd (1:51.888)
8. Canada	13 June	Montréal-Notre Dame	11th (1:29.544)	Rtd (clutch)	18th (1:33.465)
9. Holland	3 July	Zandvoort	5th (1:15.832)	4th at 1:23.720	18th (1:21.220)
10. Great Britain	18 July	Brands Hatch	5th (1:10.638)	**1st 1:35:33.812**	4th (1:13.639)
11. France	25 July	Paul Ricard	9th (1:37.778)	8th at 1 lap	7th (1:43.866)
12. Germany	8 August	Hockenheim	Injured in qualifying	-	-
13. Austria	15 August	Österreichring	10th (1:32.131)	5th at 1 lap	12th (1:37.252)
14. Switzerland	29 August	Dijon-Prenois	4th (1:02.984)	3rd at 1:00.343	19th (1:08.453)
15. Italy	12 September	Monza	10th (1:32.782)	Rtd (road-holding/brakes)	13th (1:36.540)
16. Las Vegas	25 September	Las Vegas	13th (1:18.333)	Rtd (engine)	5th (1:20.462)

(*) Belgium: Disqualified due to car being underweight

Position in World Championship: 5th / 30 points
2 victories, 1 fastest lap
Average points per race for season: 1.875

1983_ McLaren MP4C-Ford Cosworth from Brazil to Austria
McLaren MP4E-TAG Porsche from Holland to South Africa

Tyres Michelin

GRAND PRIX		CIRCUIT	QUALIFYING	RESULT	RACE LAP
1. Brazil	13 March	Rio-Jacarepaguà	9th (1:36.054)	3rd at 51.883	4th (1:41.163)
2. United States West	27 March	Long Beach	23rd (1:30.188)	2nd at 27.993	MTC (1:28.330)
3. France	17 April	Paul Ricard	11st (1:41.065)	Rtd (wheel bearing)	10th (1:45.974)
4. San Marino	1st May	Imola	17th (1:36.099)	Rtd (accident)	13th (1:38.641)
5. Monaco	15 May	Monaco	NQ (1:29.898)	-	-
6. Belgium	22 May	Spa-Francorchamps	15th (2:09.475)	Rtd (engine)	13th (2:10.899)
7. United States East	5 June	Detroit	18th (1:48.992)	Rtd (damper)	17th (1:51.318)
8. Canada	12 June	Montréal-Notre Dame	19th (1:33.671)	Rtd (accident)	22nd (1:36.071)
9. Great Britain	16 July	Silverstone	15th (1:14.267)	6th at 1 lap	11st (1:15.923)
10. Germany	7 August	Hockenheim	18th (1:56.730)	Disqualified *	11st (1:57.297)
11. Austria	14 August	Österreichring	14th (1:34.518)	6th at 2 laps	11st (1:37.552)
12. Holland	28 August	Zandvoort	19th (1:20.131)	Rtd (brakes)	15th (1:22.462)
13. Italy	11 September	Monza	13rd (1:33.133)	Rtd (electrics)	15th (1:37.132)
14. Europe	25 September	Brands Hatch	13rd (1:13.972)	Rtd (engine)	16th (1:15.957)
15. South Africa	15 October	Kyalami	12nd (1:07.974)	Rtd (electrics) 11st	2nd (1:10.634)

(*) Germany: Disqualified after backing up in the pit lane.

Position in World Championship: 10th / 12 points
1 fastest lap
Average per race: 0.666

1984_ McLaren MP4/2-TAG Porsche all season

Tyres Michelin

GRAND PRIX		CIRCUIT	QUALIFYING	RESULT	RACE LAP
1. Brazil	25 March	Rio-Jacarepaguà	6th (1:29.854)	Rtd (electrics)	5th (1:38.389)
2. South Africa	7 April	Kyalami	8th (1:06.043)	**1st 1:29:23.430**	4th (1:09.666)
3. Belgium	29 April	Zolder	13rd (1:18.071)	Rtd (water pump)	10th (1:21.853)
4. San Marino	6 May	Imola	5th (1:30.325)	Rtd (engine)	13rd (1:34.686)
5. France	20 May	Dijon-Prenois	9th (1:04.419)	**1st 1:31:11.951**	2nd (1:06.100)
6. Monaco	3 June	Monaco	7th (1:23.886)	Rtd (tête at queue)	11st (1:56.993)
7. Canada	17 June	Montréal-Notre Dame	7th (1:27.392)	2nd at 2.612	2nd (1:29.083)
8. United States East	24 June	Detroit	9th (1:43.484)	Rtd (electronics)	8th (1:47.192)
9. Dallas	8 July	Dallas	5th (1:37.987)	Rtd (accident)	MTC (1:45.353)
10. Great-Britain	22 July	Brands Hatch	3rd (1:11.344)	**1st 1:29:28.532**	MTC (1:13.191)
11. Germany	5 August	Hockenheim	7th (1:48.912)	2nd at 3.149	2nd (1:53.778)
12. Austria	19 August	Österreichring	4th (1:26.715)	**1st 1:21:12.851**	MTC (1:32.882)
13. Holland	26 August	Zandvoort	6th (1:14.866)	2nd at 10.283	3rd (1:20.470)
14. Italy	9 September	Monza	4th (1:28.533)	**1st 1:20:29.065**	MTC (1:31.912)
15. Europe	7 October	Nürburgring	15th (1:22.643)	4th at 43.086	3rd (1:23.729)
16. Portugal	21 October	Estoril	11st (1:23.183)	2nd at 13.425	MTC (1:22.996)

World Championship classification:
World Champion / 72 points
5 victories, 5 fastest race laps.
Points average per race: 4.5

1985 _McLaren MP4/2B-TAG Porsche all season

Tyres Michelin

	GRAND PRIX		CIRCUIT	QUALIFYING	RESULT	RACE LAP
1.	Brazil	7 April	Rio-Jacarepaguà	9th (1:29.984)	Rtd (fuel feed)	3rd (1:38.098)
2.	Portugal	21 April	Estoril	7th (1:23.288)	Rtd (engine)	9th (1:46.633)
3.	San Marino	5 May	Imola	7th (1:28.399)	4th at 1 lap	7th (1:32.198)
4.	Monaco	19 May	Monaco	14th (1:21.907)	Rtd (spin)	11st (1:25.842)
5.	Canada	16 June	Montréal-Notre Dame	17th (1:28.126)	Rtd (engine)	12nd (1:30.433)
6.	United States East	23 June	Detroit	12nd (1:46.266)	Rtd (brakes)	15th (1:49.489)
7.	France	7 July	Paul Ricard	6th (1:33.860)	Rtd (gearbox)	8th (1:42.037)
8.	Great-Britain	21 July	Silverstone	10th (1:07.743)	Rtd (electrics)	3rd (1:10.905)
9.	Germany	4 August	Hockenheim	12nd (1:19.652)	5th at 1:13.972	**MTC (1:22.806)**
10.	Austria	18 August	Österreichring	3rd (1:26.250)	Rtd (turbo)	2nd (1:30.052)
11.	Holland	25 August	Zandvoort	10th (1:13.059)	**1st 1:32:29.263**	2nd (1:17.054)
12.	Italy	8 September	Monza	16th (1:26.715)	Rtd (transmission)	4th (1:29.998)
13.	Belgium	15 September	Spa-Francorchamps	Withdrew (injured)	-	-
14.	Europe	6 October	Brands Hatch	Withdrew (injured)	-	-
15.	South Africa	19 October	Kyalami	8th (1:04.283)	Rtd (turbo)	5th (1:09.500)
16.	Australia	3 novembre	Adelaïde	16th (1:23.941)	Rtd (accident/brakes)	4th (1:24.498)

World Championship classification: 10th / 14 points,
1 victory, 1 fastest lap
Points average: 0.875

They may have gone at it hammer and tongs on the track but off it Lauda and Fittipaldi were the best of friends.

INDEX

_ACKNOWLEDGEMENTS

The authors would like to thank the following for their help:
Jean-Pierre Beltoise, Pierre Dupasquier, Mauro Forghieri, Robin Herd, Gérard Larrousse, Niki Lauda, Max Mosley, Michel Morelli, Gordon Murray, Alain Prost, Clay Regazzoni, Patrick Tambay, John Watson.

Certain key people in Niki Lauda's career did not want to answer our questions. We respect their wishes.

_BIBLIOGRAPHY

"La course et moi"
Niki Lauda, avec Fitz Indra et Kerbert Völker – Ed. Solar

"A la limite"
Niki Lauda, avec Herbert Völker – Ed. Solar

"300 à l'heure"
Niki Lauda – Ed. Robert Laffont

"Ferrari, les monoplaces de Grand Prix"
Alan Henry – Ed. ACLA

"Brabham, les monoplaces de Grand Prix"
Alan Henry – Ed. ACLA

"McLaren", "Formule 1", "Can-Am", "Indy"
Doug Nie – Ed. ACLA

"Memoirs of Enzo Ferrari's lieutenant"
Franco Gozzi – Giorgio Nada Editore

"Autocourse" and "The Formula 1 Yearbook"

"Auto-Hebdo" and "Sport-Auto" magazines